FAST TRACK

PHONICS

For Young Adults and Adults

Teacher's Guide

Kaye Wiley

Longman

Fast Track Phonics
Teacher's Guide

Pearson Education, 10 Bank Street, White Plains, NY 10606

Vice president, editorial director: Allen Ascher
Executive editor: Anne Stribling
Senior development editor: Virginia Bernard
Vice president, director of design and production: Rhea Banker
Executive managing editor: Linda Moser
Senior production manager: Alana Zdinak
Production editor: Robert Ruvo
Cover design: Patricia Wosczyk
Director of manufacturing: Patrice Fraccio
Senior manufacturing buyer: Edie Pullman
Text design: Patricia Wosczyk
Text composition: TSI Graphics

ISBN: 0-13-091586-6
5 6 7 8 9 10–BAH–10 09 08 07 06

Meet the Phonics Team

About the Author

Kaye Wiley is an educator, curriculum developer, and writer with more than thirty years of classroom experience in the United States and abroad. She graduated from the University of California at Berkeley and completed an M.Ed. in Bilingual Education/ESL at the University of Houston, where she specialized in psycholinguistics and second-language acquisition. After beginning her career teaching middle school in Concord, California, she went to Istanbul, Turkey, where she taught at Robert College and the Istanbul Community School for ten years. In 1981, she returned to Houston with her husband and three children, and became head of the ESL Department at Awty International School. In 1991, she moved to Connecticut, where she is currently a Curriculum/Staff Developer for the New Haven Public Schools, coordinating programs in secondary ESL. Since 1997, she has also been a writer on the Connecticut State Standards Committees for both World Languages and ESL. Kaye Wiley has written three previous books—*Alligator at the Airport, Animalito Alfabeto,* and *Newcomer Phonics*—all of which emphasize emerging literacy for new language learners.

Contents ●

Introduction ••••••••••••••••••••••••••••

Fast Track Phonics is a collection of brightly illustrated phonics activities designed to help new English-language learners become confident, independent readers. The Student Book follows a careful progressive sequence, using high-frequency words in context—first with short vowels, then with blends, long vowels, digraphs, *r*-controlled vowels, and diphthongs. At the end of each phonics unit, there is a photo story or photo play, which reuses the vocabulary from the unit in new contexts, such as sports, jobs, health, and family activities. Students can read these stories together, discuss them, and perform them for their own enjoyment.

THE TEACHER'S GUIDE

You may find that students who can read in their first language will be able to proceed through the pages of *Fast Track Phonics* on their own, using the clearly illustrated examples. However, it is important to augment each lesson in the Student Book with specific oral-language support from the audiocassettes and the Teacher's Guide, since students need to hear the spoken phonics sounds. Research shows us that phonemic awareness and phonics skills are developed most effectively through systematic, explicit lessons with repeated interaction between teacher and students. It is by listening and responding to the voice of the teacher that the students learn the variations in the English sound system, practice pronunciation, and build oral background in the language.

The Teacher's Guide provides not only step-by-step lessons, oral readings, songs, and chants that strengthen this oral-language connection, but also outlines suggestions for extension activities and assessments. The six-step lesson includes:

1. Focusing on Phonemic Awareness or Building Background
2. Using the Page instruction
3. Say-It oral language practice
4. Read-It listening and rereading practice
5. Activities for All Learners that include informal oral and written assessments for students with varied learning styles
6. Write-It activities for vocabulary usage.

DESCRIPTION OF THE PROGRAM

Q *How does* **Fast Track Phonics** *help students learning to read in English?*

A *Every word is illustrated.* More than 600 brightly illustrated nouns, verbs, adjectives, and prepositions highlight the pages of the Student Book and provide visual support for new readers. Although some of these words will be familiar from conversation, ELD students often need visual cues when decoding new words in English.

Only high-frequency words are used. For newcomers in English, certain words are more necessary to learn than others. *Bus* and *run,* for example, are more useful words to master when studying the short-*u* sound than *jug* or *bun,* which students rarely encounter. In traditional phonics programs designed for native English speakers, there is often a "word-family" approach, using a wide array of low-frequency words. However, *Fast Track Phonics* uses only carefully selected, relevant, high-frequency vocabulary.

Words are presented in context, not in isolation. In contrast to traditional phonics programs that rely on lists of isolated words, *Fast Track Phonics* assumes that ELD students have a limited vocabulary base and need to derive meaning from context before they can complete exercises. Therefore, all new words are presented in relation to a picture, sentence, or story. In this way, there are three sets of cues to help newcomers decipher English text: (1) illustrations, which provide a visual context; (2) full sentences, which provide a verbal context; and (3) the characters of the Team, which provide a narrative context.

The vocabulary is highly controlled. Only words that have been previously introduced and illustrated are used in sentences and stories. Thus, as students come to the photo stories and photo plays at the end of each phonics unit, they see familiar words and can feel the satisfaction of reading the story on their own. A word list of the controlled vocabulary is included at the back of the book and in the Student Book.

Decodable text is used throughout. The units in *Fast Track Phonics* are carefully structured to emphasize the most frequent, highly regular sound–symbol relationships. It was the author's goal to make all the text as decodable as possible for ELD students. However, since some important words in English contain irregular sounds (*has* = /haz/, *who* = /hoo/), they are coded with a 🔑 icon and referenced on a pronunciation chart at the back of the Student Book. Sight words like *the* are also referenced at the back in the list of irregular words.

Phonics lessons progress systematically. Units are also designed to introduce ELD students to written English carefully, step by step. Whereas basic consonants will be familiar to many from similar sounds in their own language, English vowel sounds with their various pronunciations and spellings, as well as digraphs and diphthongs, may be new.

Syntax is simple and language structures are limited. Newcomers to English are at the early stages of language acquisition. They are progressing from silent listening to one-word utterances and short sentences. For this reason, activities and stories in *Fast Track Phonics* reinforce the following early-stage language structures:

1. Simple declarative sentences: *Pat has a hat.*
2. Present tense verbs: *go, see* (simple present tense); *is going, is seeing* (present progressive tense)
3. Negative forms: *Bud is not on the bus.*
4. Interrogative forms: *Is Bud on the bus?*

See the Scope and Sequence chart on pages viii–ix for more details.

Q *How are* **Fast Track Phonics** *units organized?*

A *Words are repeated and recycled continually.* At the end of most units there is a review page that helps students practice words from that unit plus previous words from other units. In addition, recycling of vocabulary in the context of practice sentences continues throughout the book. The photo stories and photo plays contain carefully controlled vocabulary that is cumulative as well, reviewing not only the words from the unit but also words from prior units.

ELD thematic topics are included. To make the content of lessons more relevant for ELD students, phonics activities are designed around themes such as outdoor activities, family, jobs, health, sports, and transportation. (See the Scope and Sequence chart on pages viii–ix for more details.)

Grammar topics are incorporated in exercises. Since young adult ELD students can often benefit from a more structured approach to second-language learning, topics such as verbs, pronouns, prepositions, and adjectives are also included. Notes in the Teacher's Guide provide suggestions and extension activities for these grammatical topics.

Writing and reading are presented concurrently. In line with research suggesting that coding and decoding in language (i.e. reading and writing) reinforce each other when taught together, *Fast Track Phonics* includes writing opportunities in every unit. As they learn phonics, ELD students are also practicing to write and spell with phonemes.

Q *What are the photo stories and photo plays?*

A *At the end of each unit in the Student Book there is a colorful story or play about the Phonics Team.* Each story reuses familiar words in a new context. Students enjoy listening to these stories and plays on the audiocassette, reading them aloud, and perhaps performing them together.

Q *What assessments does the program include?*

A **Fast Track Phonics** *includes both formal and informal assessments.* The Student Book contains eight written assessment/review pages—a kind of mini-quiz at the end of each unit. The Teacher's Guide similarly contains ten supplementary written assessment pages. Equally important, however, are the ongoing informal assessments that the students themselves can use as self-assessments. The Teacher's Guide also contains oral and written assessments as part of each lesson plan.

Q *What are the other components of the* **Fast Track Phonics** *program?*

A *Besides the Student Book and Teacher's Guide, there are two other valuable teaching aides in the* **Fast Track Phonics** *program: an audio program and colorful phonics cards.*

The Audio Program contains thirty-five lively chants and songs on an audiocassette. For more listening and reading practice, the photo stories and photo plays are also recorded. These chants, songs, and stories recycle key vocabulary and feature the phonics sounds from each unit, such as short vowels, long vowels, blends, digraphs, *r*-controlled vowels, and diphthongs.

Phonics Cards This set includes fifty 8" X 10" two-sided cards (more than ninety photographic and illustrated images), one for each phonic element taught in the program. Cards are categorized by ELD themes for more teaching opportunities and cross-classification. The teacher can cover words for assessment purposes.

Scope and Sequence • • • • • • • • • • •

THE FAST TRACK PHONICS PROGRAM

	PHONIC ELEMENTS	GRAMMAR TOPICS	ELD THEMES
UNIT 1	short vowels: a, o, i, final x	verbs: *has, tap, jog, hop, can, cannot, sit, hit, fit, is, is not*; prepositions: *on, off*; adjectives; possessives using *'s*	sports, household items, clothes, animals, sizes, emotions
UNIT 2	short vowels: u, e	verbs: *run, has, get*; yes/no questions; plural *s*	outdoors, colors, weather, numbers, transportation, parts of the body, food, family
UNIT 3	blends: cl, fl, pl, bl, gl, sl, gr, fr, br, tr, cr, dr, st, sp, sn, sw, sk, sm, nd, lk, mp, nk, ft, xt, st, sk, lp, lt, nt	verbs: *drop, spill, smell, swim, jump*; preposition: *next to*	school, outdoors, food, animals, transportation, weather, time, clothes, senses, colors, jobs
UNIT 4	long vowels: a	verbs: *make, take, wake, play, say, lay, wait, have*; contractions: *can't, isn't*; similar words	food, outdoor activities, landscape, animals weather, time, emotions, face, transportation
UNIT 5	long vowels: i	verbs: *ride, like, fly, cry, drive, smile, hide, bite*; pronouns: *I, my*; preposition: *by*; adjectives	recreation/bikes, numbers, time, parts of the body, day/night, left/right, rhymes, emotions, questions, lists, likes/dislikes

	PHONIC ELEMENTS	GRAMMAR TOPICS	ELD THEMES
UNIT 6	long vowels: o, e, u	verbs: *hold, float, go, grow, blow, read, study, sleep, eat, hear, see, use*; adjectives; pronouns: *he, me, you*; prepositions; *in back of, behind, beside, below, between, above, in front of*; questions with *do you*; contraction: *don't*	sports, games, food, household objects, weather, months, outdoors, temperature, trees, colors , animals, numbers, many/few, opposites, parts of the body, time, emotions, riddles, musical instruments
UNIT 7	digraphs: sh, ph, th	verbs: *shop, wash, shave, shave, think, throw*; questions with *do you*; preposition: *with*; demonstrative pronouns and adjectives: *this, that, these, those,*	transportation, telephone, clothes, colors, baby-sitting, animals, parts of the body, math, graphs, outdoor activities, rhymes
UNIT 8	digraphs: wh, ng, ch, tch, wr, kn	verbs: *sing, catch, watch, pitch, write, know*; questions with *what*; questions with *when*; adjectives; present progressive verbs; homonyms	weather, animals, numbers, time, school, health, safety, doctor, months, lunch, math, utensils, outdoors, thinking/imagining, sports, songs, right/wrong, riddles, rhymes
UNIT 9	r-controlled vowels: ar, er, ir, ur	prepositions: *over/under, before/after*; verbs: *are, hurt, wear*	farm, family, outdoors, weather, seasons, clothes, colors, parts of the body, safety, animals, time, transportation, numbers
UNIT 10	diphthongs: oo, ou, ow, oy, oi	verbs: *shoot, bounce, dance, boil*; adjectives; preposition: *around*; questions with *how*; expressions: *cool*	house, rooms, furniture, town, noises, music, school, clothes, toys, sports, animals, riddles, parts of the body, colors, days of the week, exclamations, parties/celebrations

UNIT 1

Short Vowels: a, o, i

Short Vowels: /a/ a

New Words: Pat, has, bat, cap, cat, map, hat, bag, pan, man, mat, van, tap, fat

---

Phonics Objectives

Can students:
- ✓ listen for /a/ as in *Pat*?
- ✓ identify the short-*a* vowel sound?
- ✓ read and write the letter *a* in words and sentences?

Language Acquisition Objectives

Students:
- use the verbs *has, tap*

ESL Standards
- Goal 2, Standard 1

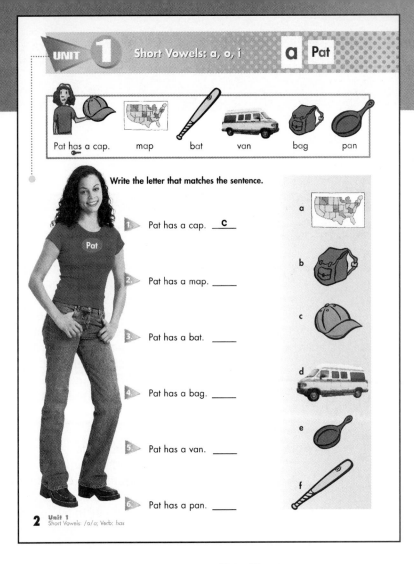

FOCUSING ON PHONEMIC AWARENESS

Point out and pronounce objects in the class that have the short-*a* sound such as a *map*, a *cap*, a *bag*, and a *hand*. Say the word *map* and model oral blending: *m-a-p*. Invite students to practice, slowly blending the sounds in the other words with you. Then ask them to tell you how the words are alike. (/a/ sound)

Display picture cards of objects such as a *pan*, a *cat*, a *map*, a *man*, *Pat*, and a *van*. Pass these around and ask students to say the words. Listen to students' pronunciation and correct them, asking them to repeat the word if necessary.

Say the following words and ask students to raise their hands when they hear a word with the short-*a* sound: *hop, map, hill, bat, sit, bag*, and *Pat*.

USING THE PAGES

Page 2

Ask students to:
- point to letter *a* that stands for /a/
- listen as you read words in box
- locate words as you repeat them
- read aloud and track words with you

Direct students' attention to the box at the top of the page. Read aloud the example sentence *Pat has a cap*. Point out the pronunciation key icon under the word *has*. Explain that students can look up the pronunciation of any words that appear with this icon by referring to the Irregular Words at the end of their Student Books.

Point out the photo of Pat on p. 2 and the illustrations of Pat on pp. 2–3. Explain that each Phonics Team character appears both in photos and cartoons.

Page 3

Ask students to:
- point to letter *a* that stands for /a/
- listen as you read words in box
- locate words as you repeat them
- read aloud and track words with you

Read together: "*Pat has . . .* " Ask a student to role-play Pat. Give that student a picture of a cat and say, *Pat has a cat*. Give another student a map and say (*name of student*) *has a map; Pat has a cat*. Switch objects and ask the class, *Who has a cat? Who has a map?* You can continue the activity with other short-*a* objects and students.

Read the sentence *Pat taps a bat* and demonstrate the verb *taps* by tapping a pencil on a desk. Point out *a fat cat*, as an illustration in the top box.

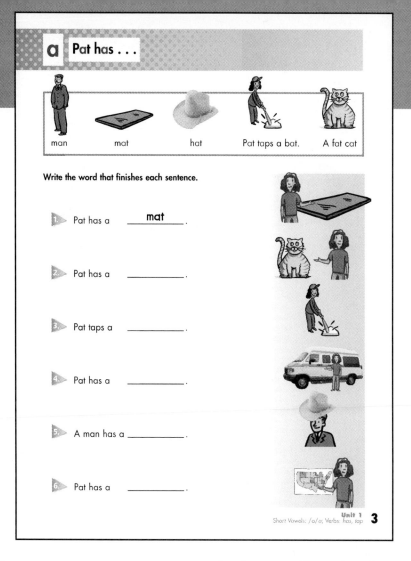

a | **Pat has . . .**

man   mat   hat   Pat taps a bat.   A fat cat

Write the word that finishes each sentence.

1. Pat has a ___mat___ .

2. Pat has a _____ .

3. Pat taps a _____ .

4. Pat has a _____ .

5. A man has a _____ .

6. Pat has a _____ .

ACTIVITIES FOR ALL LEARNERS

Words-in-the-Envelope Game
(Kinesthetic Learners)

Object of the game: To pull out a word card from a large envelope, read it, pronounce it, and use it in a sentence.

Materials: a large manila envelope, index cards or picture cards with short-*a* words on them. (*map, bag, man*)

Directions: Emphasize the short-*a* sound as you explain the game, showing the envelope and word cards in it. Ask students to take turns and do the following:

(1) pull out a card; (2) read the short-*a* word on the card aloud; (3) use the name of a person in the class to make a sentence with that word, adding the verb *has*, for example: *Jose has a ____* (*name of object on card*).

Model the first example for them, pulling out an *a*-word (*map*) and naming the student next to you to make the sentence

Jose has a map. Give students the opportunity to find other objects in the room that have the short-*a* sound (*chalkboard, hand*, etc.).

Make a Collage
(Visual Learners)

Materials: old magazines and mail-order catalogs, scissors, glue, white paper

Directions:
Ask students to (1) find pictures of short-*a* words they know (*hat, van*); (2) cut out the pictures; (3) design a collage by pasting the short-*a* pictures on paper.

Have students tell a partner about pictures they put in their collage.

Song: "This Land Is Your Land"
(Auditory Learners)

Play the audiocassette of the song "This Land Is Your Land." Distribute copies of the lyrics on p. 93 and invite students to follow along as you read aloud. Explain any words that the students do not understand. (*redwood forest, gulf stream waters*) Have the students read the words

aloud with you, line by line. Have them circle the short-*a* sounds. (*land, California, island*)

Play the audiocassette again, this time inviting the students to sing along. Ask them to listen for all the short-*a* sounds. Ask students to name popular songs they know that contain short-*a* words. Suggest that they bring in their tapes or CDs of these songs and play them for the class.

Find an *a*-word in the Newspaper (*van, man, hat . . .*)
(Extra Reading)

Materials: newspapers, writing paper, pens

Directions: Divide students into groups. Invite each group to look in newspapers and (1) find words that contain the short-*a* sound; (2) list them on a paper; (3) copy the sentences, captions, or titles that include the *a*-words under each word. At the end of ten minutes, the group having the longest list of *a*-words is the winner.

Read It!

Play the audiocassette of p. 3. Have students (1) read along and listen to the following lines and (2) repeat them as directed. Check pronunciation of the sound *a* carefully as students repeat the lines.

    man   mat   hat
    Pat taps a bat.
    A fat cat
1. Pat has a mat.
2. Pat has a cat.
3. Pat taps a bat.
4. Pat has a van.
5. A man has a hat.
6. Pat has a map.

Write It!
Dictation

Say the focus words: *Pat, has, bat, cap, cat, map, hat, bag, pan, man, mat, van, tap, fat*. Ask students to write each of the words as you repeat them. At the end of the dictation, have the students exchange papers and correct their written work.

Short Vowels: /o/ o

New Words: Tom, jog, hop, dog, on, off, rock, mop, pot, can, cannot

Phonics Objectives

Can students:
- ✓ listen for /o/ as in *Tom*?
- ✓ identify the short-*o* vowel sound?
- ✓ read and write the letter *o* in words and sentences?

Language Acquisition Objectives

Can students:
- ✓ use the verbs *jog*, *hop*, *can/cannot*?
- ✓ use the prepositions *on* and *off*?

ESL Standards
- Goal 1, Standard 3

Focusing on Phonemic Awareness

Display pictures of three or four objects that have the short-*o* sound in them. These may include a *rock*, a *pot*, a *mop*, and a *dog*. Raise each picture and pronounce its name for the students. Model oral blending. For example, say the word *rock*: *r-o-ck*. Invite students to pronounce the words after you. Then ask the students to tell you how the names for the items are alike. (/o/ sound)

Keeping the short-*o* pictures on display, add a few other pictures that do not have the short-*o* sound. In a random order, pick up the pictures one at a time. Challenge the students to raise their hands when you lift a picture that has the short-*o* sound.

Using the Pages

Page 4

Ask students to:
- point to letter *o* that stands for /o/
- listen as you read words in box
- locate words as you repeat them
- read aloud and track words with you

Ask students to look at the sentence *Tom can jog* and its illustration in the box. Read the sentence aloud and demonstrate the verb *jog*. Then point to the sentence *Tom hops* and its illustration, read it aloud, and demonstrate the verb *hops*.

Direct students' attention to the illustrations of *the hat on the rock* and *the hat off the rock* in the box. Then demonstrate the prepositions *on* and *off* with objects in the class. Have students repeat the demonstration and describe the position of the object, for example *The pencil is on/off the desk.*

Page 5

Ask students to:
- point to letter *o* that stands for /o/
- listen as you read words in box
- locate words as you repeat them
- read aloud and track words with you

Point out the words *can* and *cannot* at the top of the page and ask the class to repeat them after you. Ask, *Which word has the short-*o* sound?*

Request that a student stand up and jog. Say, *(name of student) can jog*. Invite the class to repeat the sentence. Next, ask the student to fly. Say, *(name of student) cannot fly*. Have the class repeat the sentence. You can repeat this with other actions that students can and cannot do.

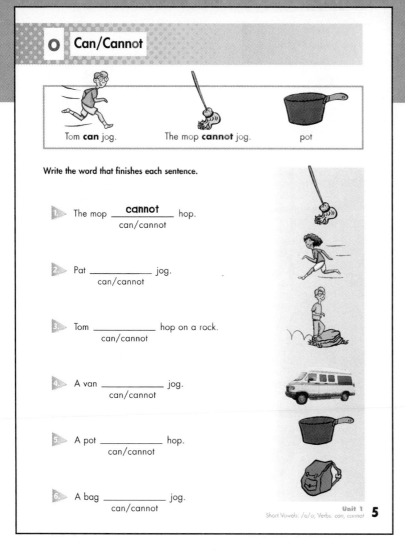

o Can/Cannot

Tom **can** jog.   The mop **cannot** jog.   pot

Write the word that finishes each sentence.

1. The mop ___**cannot**___ hop.
   can/cannot

2. Pat _____ jog.
   can/cannot

3. Tom _____ hop on a rock.
   can/cannot

4. A van _____ jog.
   can/cannot

5. A pot _____ hop.
   can/cannot

6. A bag _____ jog.
   can/cannot

Short Vowels: /o/o; Verbs: can, cannot   **Unit 1 5**

Extension activity: If a kitchen or electric crock pot is available, you might try to make real soup in the pot. Divide students into groups. Each group prepares a different item for the soup (peel potatoes, chop celery or onions). Students then describe what they have done and copy the recipe.

Say It!

Play the audiocassette of the following chant:

I can hop. Hop, hop, hop!
I can jog. Jog, jog, jog!
I can mop. Mop, mop, mop.
But I'm hot! Hot, hot, hot!

Distribute copies of the chant on p. 93. Have students underline words containing the short-*o* sound. Choose some words to model orally, blending the sounds together, such as: *h-o-p*. As the class repeats the chant, ask for volunteers to perform the actions indicated.

Write It!

On the chalkboard, write the following sentences:

A man can _____.
A van cannot _____.
A dog can _____.
A pot cannot _____.
A cat can _____.
A mat cannot _____.

Ask students to (1) think of short-*o* words or short-*a* words to complete the sentences; (2) copy the sentences; (3) add two more original sentences of their own.

ACTIVITIES FOR ALL LEARNERS

Charades
(Kinesthetic Learners)

Materials: slips of paper with short-*o* or short-*a* words written on them (i.e. *jog, mop, rock, pot, hop, cat, pan, hat, man,* etc.)

Directions: Divide the class into two teams. Explain that members of each team will take turns acting out the word that they select, for example *jog*, and the other team will try to guess the word.

Read It!

Play the audiocassette of p. 5. Have students (1) read along and listen to the following lines and (2) repeat them as directed. Check pronunciation of the sound *o* carefully as students repeat the lines.

Tom can jog.
The mop cannot jog.
pot
1. The mop cannot hop.
2. Pat can jog.
3. Tom can hop on a rock.
4. A van cannot jog.
5. A pot cannot hop.
6. A bag cannot jog.

In the Pot
(Visual/Kinesthetic Learners)

Materials: cooking pot, spoon

Directions: Pantomime a cooking lesson and describe what you would put in the pot to make soup (or spaghetti sauce, etc.). Ask students what they would add next. This is a good way to review food vocabulary, especially vegetables and meat, and it often prompts conversation about foods from different cultures.

Short Vowels: /i/ i

New Words: Will, sit, hill, hit, is, fit, mitt, big, little

Focusing on Phonemic Awareness

As you sit down on a chair, say the word *sit*. Repeat the word *sit* slowly, stressing the sounds *s-i-t*. Have the students repeat the word *sit*. Listen to be sure they are pronouncing the short-*i* correctly. Point to the seat of the chair, noting that the word *seat* (long-*e* sound) is pronounced differently than the verb *sit* (short-*i* sound). Many ESL students have difficulty with this distinction. Say the following words and ask students to raise their hand when they hear a word with the short-*i* sound in it: *top, tip, pot, pit, mitt, has, his, at, is.*

Using the Pages

Page 6

Ask students to:
• point to letter *i* that stands for /i/
• listen as you read words in box
• locate words as you repeat them
• read aloud and track words with you

Invite the class to examine the illustrations in the box. Ask a volunteers to (1) stand and then sit; (2) pretend to hit a ball with a bat; (3) fit an imaginary hat on a head or fit a mitt on a hand. Point to the sentence *Will sits on a hill* and read it aloud. Ask, *Which three words have the /i/ sound?* (*Will, sits, hill*) Repeat this activity with the other sentences in the box.

Page 7

Ask students to:
• point to letter *i* that stands for /i/
• listen as you read words in box
• locate words as you repeat them
• read aloud and track words with you

Pronounce the words *is* and *is not* and invite the class to repeat them after you. Ask the class to look at the first picture in the box and point to the picture of the big dog. Say, *is big*, and have them pronounce the phrase with you. Repeat this with the other three pairs of illustrations in the box.

i | Is/Is Not

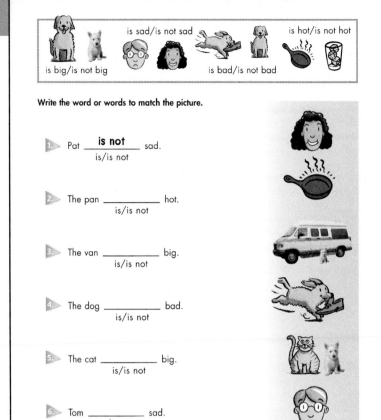

is big/is not big   is sad/is not sad   is bad/is not bad   is hot/is not hot

Write the word or words to match the picture.

1. Pat __is not__ sad.
   is/is not

2. The pan _____ hot.
   is/is not

3. The van _____ big.
   is/is not

4. The dog _____ bad.
   is/is not

5. The cat _____ big.
   is/is not

6. Tom _____ sad.
   is/is not

Short Vowels: /i/ i; Verbs: is, is not; Adjectives   **Unit 1 7**

ACTIVITIES FOR ALL LEARNERS

Simon Says: Verbs
(TPR—Total Physical Response—or Kinesthetic Learners)

Ask the class to stand. Review the rules of the game Simon Says: (1) Listen very carefully as you say different verb commands (*Simon says hop*). (2) Copy the action only if the phrase "Simon says" precedes the command. (3) If a student mimics the action without the phrase "Simon says," the student must sit down. The last one standing is the winner. Examples: *Simon says jog. Simon says sit. Simon says tap a bag. Hit a ball* (no "Simon says"). *Simon says hop. Simon says fit a hat. Simon says he is sad* (sad face), etc. Ask students for other verbs they know and list them on the board. Repeat the game using their verbs as well as those above. You can make the game more difficult by asking students to repeat each phrase after you.

Sentence Strips: Short-*i* Words
(Visual/Kinesthetic Learners)

Object:

(1) To have students make new sentences using short-*i* words and review short-*o* and short-*a* words from previous units.

(2) To assess student comprehension of vocabulary and sounds.

Materials: strips of blank construction paper, index cards with words from the lesson copied onto them; students can make packets of their own cards.

Directions: Using words from Unit 1, dictate new sentences to the students. Ask them to arrange the words on the colored strips, for example: *Will sits on a rock. The van is on a hill. Pat has a mitt. The dog is not big. Will is sad. Tom is not mad. The pan is hot.*

Verb Collage
(Extra Help)

Materials: old magazines, catalogs and newspapers, scissors, glue, poster paper

Directions: Divide students into groups. Challenge the groups to look through the catalogs and magazines and find pictures that illustrate verbs they have learned, for example: *fits/does not fit; sits, hits, is big/is little; is sad/is not sad; is hot/is not hot, can jog/cannot jog;* etc. Distribute poster paper, scissors, and glue and have each group make a collage of cut-out verb pictures. Decorate a bulletin board with the group posters. Have students explain the verbs, stressing the short-vowel sounds.

Read It!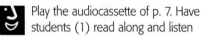

Play the audiocassette of p. 7. Have students (1) read along and listen to the following lines and (2) repeat them as directed. Check pronunciation of the sound *i* carefully as students repeat the lines.

> is big/is not big
> is sad/is not sad
> is bad/is not bad
> is hot/is not hot

1. Pat is not sad.
2. The pan is hot.
3. The van is big.
4. The dog is bad.
5. The cat is big.
6. Tom is sad.

Write It!

Photocopy page 7 and ask students to circle all the words that contain the short-*i* sound.

Creative writing: Invite one student at a time to write additional stanzas that they have created (above) on the board. Read the new stanzas together, stressing the short-*i* words. Have students copy these additional lines onto their papers and circle the short-*i* words.

Short Vowels: /a/ a, /o/ o, /i/ i

New Words: of, on, off

Phonics Objectives

Can students:
- ✓ listen for /a/ as in *Pat*, /o/ as in *Tom*, and /i/ as in *Will*?
- ✓ identify the short vowel sounds the letters *a*, *o*, and *i* stand for?
- ✓ read and write the letters *a*, *o*, and *i* in words and sentences?

Language Acquisition Objectives

Can students:
- ✓ use possessives using *'s*?
- ✓ use the prepositions *on* and *off*?

ESL Standards

- Goal 1, Standard 3

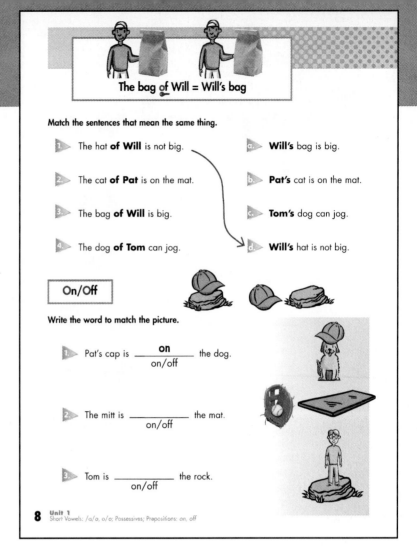

The bag of Will = Will's bag

Match the sentences that mean the same thing.

1. The hat **of Will** is not big.
2. The cat **of Pat** is on the mat.
3. The bag **of Will** is big.
4. The dog **of Tom** can jog.

a. **Will's** bag is big.
b. **Pat's** cat is on the mat.
c. **Tom's** dog can jog.
d. **Will's** hat is not big.

On/Off

Write the word to match the picture.

1. Pat's cap is ___**on**___ the dog.
   on/off
2. The mitt is _____ the mat.
   on/off
3. Tom is _____ the rock.
   on/off

BUILDING BACKGROUND

Ask a student to come forward. Hand him or her a bag and say, *This is (student's name) 's bag.* Ask the student to hand the bag to someone else and repeat the phrase, using that person's name.

Then place a hat on a desk. Ask students where the hat is. (*on the desk*) Take the hat off the desk and say, *Now the hat is off the desk.* Put it on your head, asking the students where the hat is now. (*on your head*) Remove it and ask where is it now. (*off your head*) Invite students to repeat more examples of *on* and *off* movements for the class.

USING PAGE 8

Read *The bag of Will* and *Will's bag* at the top of the page, tracking the two phrases with your finger. Explain that both phrases

mean the same thing: *The bag belongs to Will.* Point to the apostrophe in the second phrase and explain how *'s* indicates possession, that something belongs to someone or something else.

INCLUDING ALL LEARNERS

Whose Is It?
(Kinesthetic Learners)

Invite volunteers to hold up something they own. Write the corresponding pairs of phrases on the chalkboard, such as *the book of Julio = Julio's book.*

Say It!

Materials: a hat
Directions: Ask a volunteer to stand up. Hold up the hat and say, *This is (name of student) 's hat.* Place the hat on the student's head and then say, *The hat is on (name of student) 's head.* Ask the volunteer to go to another student and do

and say the same things. (Example: *This is Tina's hat. The hat is on Tina's head.*) Repeat the activity with other volunteers.

Write It!

Write the following on the board and ask students to fill in the blanks with the correct word(s):

The mitt of Will = _____
_____ = Tom's bat
The van of Pat = _____

Photo Story: "The Big Van"

Review Words: van, Pat, has, map, bag, bat, mat, bat, pan, and, bad, can, cannot, hop, Tom, dog, pot, of, on, off, Will, in, is, big, fit, sit, it

Phonics Objectives

Can students:
- ✓ listen for the /a/ as in *Pat*, /o/ as in *hop*, and /i/ as in *big*?
- ✓ read letters for short vowels *a*, *o*, and *i* in words in the context of a story?
- ✓ write words with the short vowels *a*, *o*, and *i*?

Language Acquisition Objectives

Can students:
- ✓ read and comprehend Unit 1 words in a story context?

ESL Standards

- Goal 1, Standard 2

Photo Story

The Big Van

Hop in the van, Will and Tom!

Pat has a big van.
Pat has a map.

Can you fit, Tom?

I cannot sit, Will!

The van has Pat's bag and mat in it.
It has a pot and pan in it.
It has a bat and ball in it.

Bad dog!

Tom's big dog hops in.
The dog sits in the van.

Pat, Tom, and Will fit in the van.
Tom's big dog fits in the van.
But the box and mitt and pot and mat cannot fit.

FOCUSING ON PHONEMIC AWARENESS 🎧

Invite students to listen as you recite the chant below. Ask them to listen carefully for the short vowel sounds /a/ and /i/.

Pat has a bat and a map and a pan.
Pat has a bag and a hat and a mitt.
Will it all fit in the van?
Will it all fit in the van?

USING THE AUDIOCASSETTE 🎧

Play the audiocassette of the chant above. To give students more practice, you may wish to photocopy the words on p. 93. Invite students to repeat the chant with you and then as a group on their own.

USING THE PHOTO STORY

🎧 **Preview** the photo story, "The Big Van," with your students. Allow the students time to look through the story and

examine the pictures and text. Ask students to follow along as you play the audiocassette of the story. Students may wish to track the words as the story is read.

Background discussion: Ask the students if they have ever ridden in a van or packed a van for a trip. Encourage them to relate their own personal experiences. Prompt them with additional questions about pet problems, such as *Do you have any pets? Do your pets ever do anything that makes you laugh?*

Read the photo story together. You may wish to assign volunteer readers to each part: four narrators—one for each set of caption lines under the four pictures—Pat, Will, and Tom. Listen for correct pronunciation of the short vowel sounds in the Review Words (above). Do not interrupt the story, but discuss problem words and errors in pronunciation after the reading. Model the correct pronunciations for students and ask them to repeat the words after you.

Review the story. Lead the class in a second reading of "The Big Van." This time, ask for new volunteers to read aloud. After they finish reading, ask questions focusing on the content of the story:

- Who has a van? (*Pat*)
- What is in the van? (*a bag, mat, bat, mitt, pan, pot,* and *hat*)
- What is Tom's problem? (*He thinks he can't fit in the van.*)
- What does Tom's dog do? (*hops in the van*)
- What happens at the end? (*They all fit in, but the box, mitt, pot, and mat are left behind.*)

Short Vowels: /a/ a, /o/ o, /i/ i
Review Words: van, Pat, has, map, bag, bat, mat, bat, pan, and, bad, can, cannot, hop, Tom, dog, pot, of, on, off, Will, in, is, big, fit, sit, it

Phonics Objectives

Can students:
✓ listen for /a/ as in *Pat*, /o/ as in *Tom*, and /i/ as in *Will*?
✓ identify the short vowel sounds the letters *a*, *o*, and *i* stand for?
✓ read words with the letters *a*, *o*, and *i* in sentences?

Language Acquisition Objectives

Can students:
✓ read and comprehend familiar words in a new context?
✓ respond to statements with *yes* and *no*?

ESL Standards

• Goal 2, Standard 1

BUILDING BACKGROUND

Ask students what is happening in the picture at the top of p. 10. Ask if anyone can tell what happened in the story on the previous page without turning back to look. Review the events of the photo story together.

USING PAGE 10

Have students read the sentences on p. 10 again quietly to themselves and circle *yes* if the sentence is correct or *no* if it is not. Point out that example 1, *Pat has a van*, has been done for them. Tell students they can turn back and reread the story if they need to check an answer. Recall and memory are not as important in this exercise as skimming and reading for information.

Questions

Circle *yes* if the sentence is true.
Circle *no* if the sentence is not true.

1	Pat has a van.	(yes)	no
2	A rock is in the van.	yes	no
3	Tom has a big map.	yes	no
4	Pat's bat is in the van.	yes	no
5	A cat is in the van.	yes	no
6	Will has a bag.	yes	no
7	A hat is in the van.	yes	no
8	A mop is in the van.	yes	no
9	Tom cannot sit in the van.	yes	no
10	Tom is a dog.	yes	no

10 Unit 1
Short Vowels: a, o, i

Write It!
Dictation

After a brief review, dictate the sentences to the students in reverse order, starting with sentence 10. Have students exchange papers, compare answers with the sentences in the book, and correct each other's papers. Note: This activity also serves as an assessment. You may note which vowels are causing difficulty for students through their misspellings.

CONTENT LINKS

MAPS/ATLASES
/a/ a
Hammond Scholastic World Atlas, Hammond, 2000
Atlas of the World, 8th Edition by George Phillip, Son: Oxford University Press, 2000
National Geographic Atlas of World History by Noel Grove and Daniel J. Boorstin: National Geographic Society, 1998

AMERICAN HISTORY
/a/ /o/ /i/
American Roots: U.S. Cultural History by Karen Blanchard and Christine Root: Pearson Education, 2000
America: The Early Years by Anna Uhl Chamot: Addison Wesley Publishing Co., 1987
America: After Independence by Anna Uhl Chamot: Addison Wesley Publishing Co., 1987

Review

Short Vowels: a, o, i
Introduction: Final x
New Words: fox, box, six

Phonics Objectives

Can students:
- ✓ listen for and identify /a/, /o/, /i/, /ks/?
- ✓ read and write the letters for short vowels *a, o, i,* and final *x* in words and sentences?

Language Acquisition Objectives

Students:
- respond to statements with *yes* or *no*
- use verbs *has, can, is*

ESL Standards
- Goal 2, Standard 1

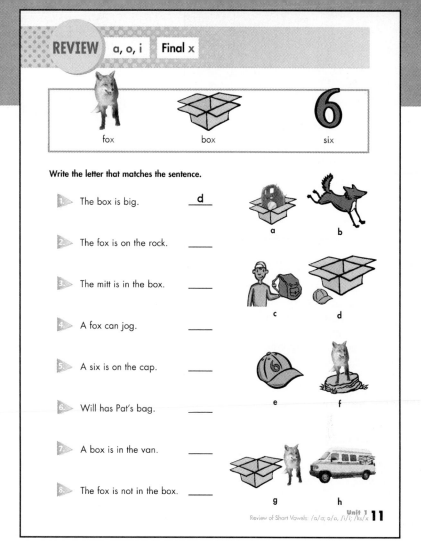

REVIEW a, o, i Final x

fox   box   six

Write the letter that matches the sentence.

1. The box is big. ___d___
2. The fox is on the rock. _____
3. The mitt is in the box. _____
4. A fox can jog. _____
5. A six is on the cap. _____
6. Will has Pat's bag. _____
7. A box is in the van. _____
8. The fox is not in the box. _____

a   b   c   d   e   f   g   h

Review of Short Vowels: /a/ a; o/ o, /i/ i; /ks/ x   **Unit 1 11**

FOCUSING ON PHONEMIC AWARENESS

Introduce final *x* by displaying a cardboard box. Have students say the word together with you. Then say these words and ask students to raise their hands when they hear a word that ends like *box*: <u>fox</u>, mop, <u>ax</u>, <u>six</u>, map, mitt, <u>ox</u>. Encourage them to think of other words that end with the same sound. (*tax, fax, fix*)

USING THE REVIEW PAGE

Ask students to:
- point to letters *a, o, i, x* that stand for /a/, /o/, /i/, /ks/
- listen as you read words in box
- locate words as you repeat them
- read aloud and track words with you

Point to the letter *a, o,* and *i* at the top of the page. Invite a volunteer to identify the letters and the sounds. Then point to final *x*. Explain that *x* is a letter that often appears at the end of words after short vowels such as *a, o,* and *i.*

Pronounce the words with final *x* in the box: *box, six.* Which sound is the same for all three words? (/ks/)

INCLUDING ALL LEARNERS

Say It!
(Auditory Learners)

Play a game with students by placing them in pairs and asking them to create sentences using words that end in final *x,* such as *The fox sat on the box* or *Max has a fax.* List their ideas on the board.

Write It!

Divide the class into pairs or small groups. Have students write six sentences with *yes/no* answers. Have them take turns reading the sentences aloud.

UNIT 2

Short Vowels: u, e

Short Vowels: /u/ u

New Words: Bud, run, bus, up, bug, mud, fun, tub, gum, rug, sun

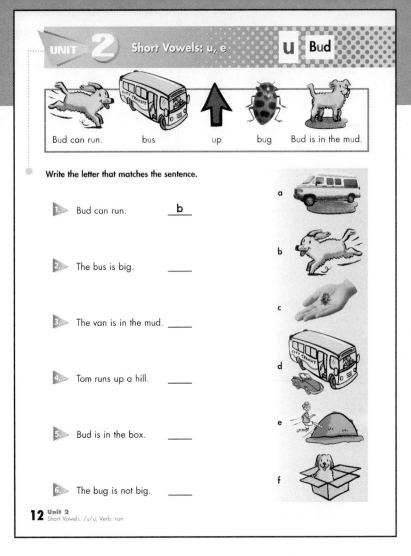

Phonics Objectives

Can students:
✓ listen for /u/ as in *Bud*?
✓ identify the short vowel sound the letter *u* stands for?
✓ read and write the letter *u* in words and sentences?

Language Acquisition Objectives

Students:
• use the verbs *run, is, sits, has*

ESL Standards
• Goal 2, Standard 1

FOCUSING ON PHONEMIC AWARENESS

Say the word *up* as you point upward. Ask the class to point up as they say the word *up* with you. Now say the word *bus*, modeling oral blending: *buuus*. Ask, *What vowel sound do you hear in the word* bus? (/u/ sound) Give an index card to each member of the class. Have students write a large letter *u* on their cards. Tell them that you are going to say a series of words. When they hear a word with the short-*u* sound, they should hold up their card. You can use the following list of paired words: *bag/bug, tab/tub, sun/fun, mad/mud, but/bat, bad/Bud.*

USING THE PAGES

Page 12

Ask students to:
• point to letter *u* that stands for /u/
• listen as you read words in box
• locate words as you repeat them
• read aloud and track words with you

Clarifying vocabulary: Point to the sentence *Bud can run* and read it aloud for the students. Ask them to repeat the sentence after you. Ask a volunteer to demonstrate the verb *run* by running in place. Then point out the sentence *Bud is in the mud* and the illustration that shows this. Ask a student to explain what *mud* is. Ask what happens if you *run* in the *mud.*

Ask students if the word *bus* is similar to a word for *bus* in their own language. (*autobus, otobus*) Building associations for English vocabulary through common cognates often helps students remember words. Again, stress the short-*u* sound in *bus*, which may be different from that of other cognates. (*oo*)

Page 13

Ask students to:
• point to letter *u* that stands for /u/
• listen as you read words in box
• locate words as you repeat them
• read aloud and track words with you

BUILDING BACKGROUND

Read the sentence *Bud has fun* aloud and invite the class to repeat it after you. Ask students what they like to do to have fun.

Have them repeat the word *gum*. Bring a pack of gum to class and hand it to a student. Say, (*student's name*) *has the gum*. Invite the class to repeat the sentence. Ask that student to hand the gum to a classmate and say, (*new student's name*) *has the gum*. If a student asks to open the package of gum, you may use the opportunity to discuss school rules about gum-chewing or whether students like to chew gum.

u Bud has fun.

Bud has fun. tub gum rug sun

Write the word that finishes each sentence.

1. Bud is in the ___tub___ .

2. Bud sits on the _____ .

3. Bud runs in the _____ .

4. Bud is in the _____ .

5. Tom has a _____ .

6. The gum is in the _____ .

Short Vowels: /u/u; Verbs: run, is, sits, has **Unit 2 13**

ACTIVITIES FOR ALL LEARNERS

On the Bus
(Kinesthetic/Auditory Learners)

Directions:

- Set up two parallel rows of chairs or desks, as on a bus.
- Put one chair (for the driver) in front of the rows.
- Ask students to guess what the set-up represents (*a bus*).
- Ask for a volunteer to be the "bus driver," and have him/her sit in the front seat. Ask the student to explain what a bus driver does (*takes money, gives transfers, announces stops*).
- Ask the others sitting in the rows to imagine why they are on the bus (*going to work, school, doctor, store*).
- Discuss the bus route and its possible stops.
- Have the students in the two rows leave their seats and stand to the side of the

class; now the bus is "empty," except for the driver.

Role-play: Begin the "bus ride." Encourage special effects from others in the class. Suggest conversation among the driver and passengers as the bus makes "stops" and people get "on/off."

After the ride: You may wish to discuss transportation modes in different countries, various customs and conditions on buses, etc. (Example: Can people bring chickens on a bus? Do people ride on the roof?)

Fun or Not Fun?
(Visual Learners)

Materials: old magazines, newspapers and catalogs, scissors, manila envelopes

Directions:

Part 1 Divide the class into groups. Give two large envelopes to each group. Ask them to write *fun* on one envelope and *not fun* on the other. Ask students to look through the magazines, catalogs, and

newspapers and cut out pictures of things that are fun or not fun. Encourage them to have fun and be creative (*babies, sports, new fashions*). Tell the students to put the sorted pictures into the appropriate envelopes. Remind them that they must agree on whether the picture is fun or not fun. Discussion is important.

Part 2 Have each group remove the pictures from their two envelopes and mix them, face down. One at a time, ask a student from each group to select a picture from the pile, hold it up, and describe it. Have the student ask the class to guess which envelope it came from, "fun" or "not fun."

Read It!
Play the audiocassette of p. 13. Have students (1) read along and listen to the following lines and (2) repeat them as directed. Check pronunciation of the sound *u* carefully as students repeat the lines.

Bud has fun.
    tub   gum   rug   sun
1. Bud is in the tub.
2. Bud sits on the mat.
3. Bud runs in the sun.
4. Bud is in the mud.
5. Tom has a bug.
6. The gum is in the box.

Write It!
Distribute writing paper to each student. One at a time, display pictures or picture cards for the short-*u* words. Ask students to (1) write down the word for each picture and (2) write a sentence using that word. Review the work as a class.

Short Vowels: /e/ e

New Words: Jen, pen, bed, red, get, net, wet, egg, seven, leg

e Jen

Jen has a pen. | bed | red | get on the bus | get off the bus

Write the letter that matches the sentence.

1. Jen has a pen. ___c___
2. Jen gets off the bus. _____
3. The cat gets on the bed. _____
4. Jen's bed is red. _____
5. Bud is on the red rug. _____
6. The big pen is red. _____

a
b
c
d
e
f

14 Unit 2
Short Vowels: /e/ e; Verb: get; Adjective: red

FOCUSING ON PHONEMIC AWARENESS

Hold up a red pen and say *red pen*, stressing the short-*e* sound. Model blending the sounds in the words together. Invite the class to say *red pen* after you.

Make sure that all students have a pen. Tell them that you are going to read some words aloud. If the word has the short-*e* sound, they are to raise their pens. Read a list of words, some of which have the short-*e* sound, such as *bug, ten, hot, hit, red, pen, men, cat, seven,* and *test*.

To extend this activity, randomly display pictures for words with and without the short-*e* sound. When the students see a picture with a name that has the short-*e* sound, they can say the word and raise their pens.

USING THE PAGES

Page 14

Ask students to:
- point to letter *e* that stands for /e/
- listen as you read words in box
- locate words as you repeat them
- read aloud and track words with you

Point to the phrases *get on the bus* and *get off the bus*. Ask students what other things they *get on* and *get off* (*train, ladder, stage,* etc.). Ask students what new words and review words can combine to make new sentences. (Example: *Jen gets on a red bus. Jen has a red bed.*) Have students write these sentences on the board.

Page 15

Ask students to:
- point to letter *e* that stands for /e/
- listen as you read words in box
- locate words as you repeat them
- read aloud and track words with you

Read the title aloud, *Is Jen . . . ?* and have the class repeat it after you. Explain that the verb *is* can be placed at the beginning of a sentence to indicate a question. Suggest a few words that may complete the question (*Is Jen a man?*). Invite volunteers to provide other words that could form a question.

Read the first word, *net,* aloud and ask students to look at the picture. Have someone explain what this kind of a *net* is used for (*basketball*). Discuss the meanings of the other short-*e* words in the box.

e | Is Jen . . . ?

net   wet dog   egg   seven   leg

Circle *yes* or *no* to answer the questions.

1. Is Jen's leg on the rock?   yes   (no)
2. Is Jen in a van?   yes   no
3. Can a bed run?   yes   no
4. Is the cat wet?   yes   no
5. Is the egg in the pan?   yes   no
6. Is the net up?   yes   no

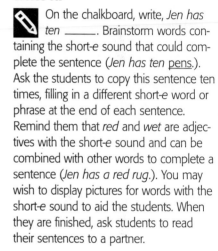

ACTIVITIES FOR ALL LEARNERS

Clap on Sevens
(Kinesthetic/Auditory Learners)

Write the numeral 7 on the board. Ask a volunteer to write the name of this numeral beside it. Explain that the word *seven* has two short-*e* sounds in it. Ask if students know other numbers with the short-*e* sound (*ten, twenty, seventeen, seventy*).

Directions: Explain that students are about to play a game called Clap on Seven. Whenever they hear the word *seven*—or a multiple of *seven*—they should clap. Ask them to count with you slowly as you demonstrate: 1, 2, 3, 4, 5, 6, (clap), 8, 9, 10, 11, 12, 13, (clap) . . . Be sure they understand the multiples of *seven* (7, 14, 21, 28, etc.). Also ask which numbers have the word *seven* in them (17, 27, 37, etc.). Point to the first person in the first row and ask that person to say *one*, the second person to say *two*, etc.

Continue down the rows until you reach *seven*. Be sure that person claps instead of saying *seven*. Have students continue counting and clapping on *sevens* and multiples of *seven*. This game is a good way to check who knows their numbers (and their multiplication tables) in English.

Name Search
(Visual Learners)

Materials: Newspapers or telephone directories, pens, paper

Directions: Write the name *Ed Lopez* on the chalkboard and point out the short-*e* sounds. Ask if there are any first or last names in the class which have the short-*e* sound in them (*Jessica, Alex*, etc.). Write the names on the chalkboard. Divide the class into pairs or small groups and distribute newspapers or telephone directories. Challenge the students to find full names of people that include the short-*e* sound. Ask them to list the names they find. When they are finished, invite each group to read their lists to the rest of the class.

Read It!

Play the audiocassette of p. 15. Have students (1) read along and listen to the following lines and (2) repeat them as directed. Check pronunciation of the sound *e* carefully as students repeat the lines.

net wet dog egg seven leg

1. Is Jen's leg on the rock?   No.
2. Is Jen in a van?   Yes.
3. Can a bed run?   No.
4. Is the cat wet?   Yes.
5. Is the egg in the pan?   No.
6. Is the net up?   Yes.

Write It!

On the chalkboard, write, *Jen has ten _____*. Brainstorm words containing the short-*e* sound that could complete the sentence (*Jen has ten* pens.). Ask the students to copy this sentence ten times, filling in a different short-*e* word or phrase at the end of each sentence. Remind them that *red* and *wet* are adjectives with the short-*e* sound and can be combined with other words to complete a sentence (*Jen has a red rug.*). You may wish to display pictures for words with the short-*e* sound to aid the students. When they are finished, ask students to read their sentences to a partner.

Short Vowels: /a/ a, /o/ o, /i/ i, /u/ u, /e/ e

Phonics Objectives

Can students:
✓ listen for /a/, /o/, /i/, /u/, and /e/?
✓ identify the short vowel sounds the letters a, o, i, u, and e stand for?
✓ read and write the letters a, o, i, u, and e in words and sentences?

Language Acquisition Objectives

Can students:
✓ add s to nouns to form plurals?

ESL Standards
• Goal 1, Standard 1

A Pen   Lots of Pens

Write the word or words to match the picture.

| a pen, ~~pens~~ |
| a cat, cats |
| an egg, eggs |
| a hat, hats |
| a bed, beds |
| a dog, dogs |
| a leg, legs |
| a bug, bugs |
| a bag, bags |
| a net, nets |

1. pens
2. _____
3. _____
4. _____
5. _____
6. _____
7. _____
8. _____

BUILDING BACKGROUND

Draw one stick figure to represent one (singular) student and two stick figures to represent two (plural) students. Point to the one student, saying, *one student*, and to the two students, saying, *two students*. Emphasize the final /s/ sound in *students*. What is the difference in the two words: *student* and *students*? Explain that the letter *s* is often added to the end of a word to show the plural form, that is, more than one. Ask students how they form plural endings to words in their own languages. Have them write their singular and plural forms on the board.

USING PAGE 16

Ask students to:
• point to letter *e* that stands for /e/
• listen as you read words in box
• locate words as you repeat them
• read aloud and track words with you

Point to the pen in the top box. Is there one pen or more than one pen? Have the students look at the second illustration. Read *lots of pens* aloud to the class and ask the students to repeat it. Point out that the word *a* signifies *one* and does not appear before the plural, *pens*. Review the pairs of singular and plural words in the box, pointing out the *a* (*an*) before the singular words and the plural *s*.

ACTIVITIES FOR ALL LEARNERS

Eggs, Eggs, Eggs
(Kinesthetic/Auditory Learners)

Materials: Index cards, pens, a real hard-boiled egg or picture of an egg

Directions: Ask the students if they know what a "recipe" is. Show them the egg and ask them what kinds of food people make with eggs in their country. Explain that you are going to write the recipe for scrambled eggs, a popular breakfast dish in the United States. Write the following

recipe on the chalkboard. Ask the students to copy it on their card and try it at home:

Ingredients: 6 eggs, milk, butter or margarine, Parmesan cheese, salt and pepper

Cookware: a bowl, a fork, a frying pan, a spatula

Directions: In a bowl, mix together with a fork: 6 eggs, 6 tbsp. milk, 1/4 cup grated Parmesan cheese, salt and pepper to taste

Melt 3 tbsp. butter or margarine in a frying pan, and pour the egg mixture into the pan with the melted butter. Stir with a spatula until eggs are cooked and dry. Serve with toast.

Write It!

Ask students to look back at vocabulary words from Unit 1. Ask them to write five sentences using plural forms of the words (*dogs, vans*) from previous lessons and read them to a partner (*Tom has lots of dogs.*). You may wish to explain that certain words ending in *x* and *s* require *es* in the plural (*boxes, buses*).

Review Words: sun, up, bus, but, mud, Bud, run, rug, Jen, bed, leg, egg, wet

Phonics Objectives

Can students:

✓ listen for the short vowel sounds /a/, /o/, /i/, /u/, and /e/?
✓ read letters for short vowels in words in the context of a story?
✓ write words with short vowels?

Language Acquisition Objectives

Can students:

✓ read words in a story context?
✓ use the verbs *is, is not, can, cannot, hops up, hops off, hits, runs, has, sit*?

ESL Standards

• Goal 1, Standard 2

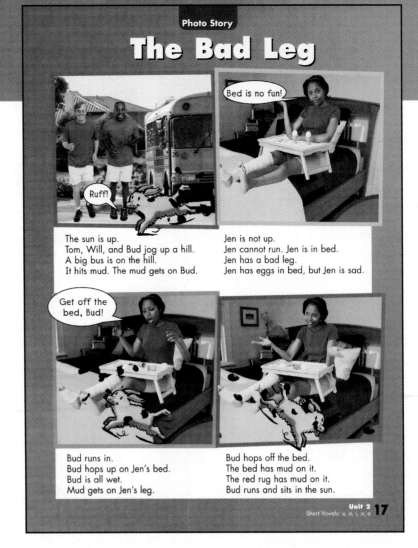

Photo Story

The Bad Leg

Ruff!

The sun is up.
Tom, Will, and Bud jog up a hill.
A big bus is on the hill.
It hits mud. The mud gets on Bud.

Bed is no fun!

Jen is not up.
Jen cannot run. Jen is in bed.
Jen has a bad leg.
Jen has eggs in bed, but Jen is sad.

Get off the bed, Bud!

Bud runs in.
Bud hops up on Jen's bed.
Bud is all wet.
Mud gets on Jen's leg.

Bud hops off the bed.
The bed has mud on it.
The red rug has mud on it.
Bud runs and sits in the sun.

Unit 2 17
Short Vowels: u, e, i, a, o

FOCUSING ON PHONEMIC AWARENESS

(Auditory Learners)

Teach the class this two-part chant. Ask them to listen for the short-*e* vowel sounds.

Group 1: Hey, Jen! . . . Jen! Can you jog?
Group 2: Jog? I can't jog.
Group 1: Why not?
Group 2: I'm in bed.
Group 1: Bed?
Group 2: I have a bad leg.
Group 1: Bad leg?
Group 2: Yes.
Group 1: You're stuck in bed?
Group 2: Yes, and I'm MAD!

USING THE AUDIOCASSETTE

Play the audiocassette of the chant. To give students more practice, you may wish to photocopy the words on p. 94. Invite students to repeat the chant with you,

then say it again on their own. Have them circle words on the photocopy of the chant that have short-*e* sound in them. (*Jen, leg, bed*)

USING THE PHOTO STORY

Preview the photo story, "The Bad Leg," with your students. Allow the students time to look through the story and examine the pictures and text. Ask students to follow along as you play the audiocassette of the story. Students may wish to track the words as the story is read.

Background discussion: Ask the students if they have ever had a bad leg or had to stay in bed for health reasons. Encourage them to relate their own personal experiences. Prompt them with additional questions about injuries. Then ask them about mischievous pets, such as *Do pets ever cause problems in your house?*

Read the photo story together. You may wish to assign volunteer readers to each part: four narrators—one for each set of caption lines under the four pictures—Bud,

and Jen. As students read, listen for correct pronunciation of the short vowel sounds in the Review Words (above). Do not interrupt the story, but discuss problem words and errors in pronunciation after the reading. Model the correct pronunciations for students and ask them to repeat the words after you.

Review the story. Lead the class in a second reading of "The Bad Leg." This time, ask for new volunteers to read aloud. After they finish reading, ask questions focusing on the content of the story:

• Who is jogging? (*Tom, Will, and Bud*)
• Who is in bed? (*Jen*)
• What is Jen's problem? (*She has a bad leg.*)
• What is Jen eating? (*an egg*)
• Is Jen happy or sad? (*sad*)
• What does the bus do? (*It gets mud on Bud.*)
• What does Bud do? (*He runs in and hops up on Jen's bed.*)
• What does Bud do at the end? (*He runs off to sit in the sun.*)

Short Vowels: /u/ u, /e/ e

Review Words: sun, up, bus, but, mud, Bud, run, rug, Jen, bed, leg, egg, wet, hill, is, in, not, dog, jogs, Tom, has, cannot, hops, the, all

Phonics Objectives

Can students:

✓ listen for /u/ as in *sun*, /e/ as in *Jen*?

✓ identify the short vowel sounds /a/, /o/, /i/, /u/, and /e/?

✓ read and write letters for short vowels *a, o, i, u,* and *e* in words and sentences?

Language Acquisition Objectives

Students:

• review verbs *is, runs, has, jogs, hops* and prepositions *on, off, in*

• use words relating to the outdoors

• read and comprehend familiar words in a new context

ESL Standards

• Goal 2, Standard 1

BUILDING BACKGROUND

Ask students what is happening in the picture at the top of p. 18. Ask students to talk about what each character is doing. Can they retell what happened in the story on the previous page without turning back to look? Invite students to talk about different things they do outdoors. Review the events of the photo story together.

USING PAGE 18

Read the instructions at the top of p. 18 to the students. Review what is happening in the pictures. Invite a volunteer to read the words in the box under the pictures. Explain that these are words from the story. Ask a student to read the example sentence, *The sun is up*. Suggest that, as students read each sentence, they try to remember the story and complete the sentence with an appropriate word from the box. If they need to check an answer, they can turn back and reread p. 17.

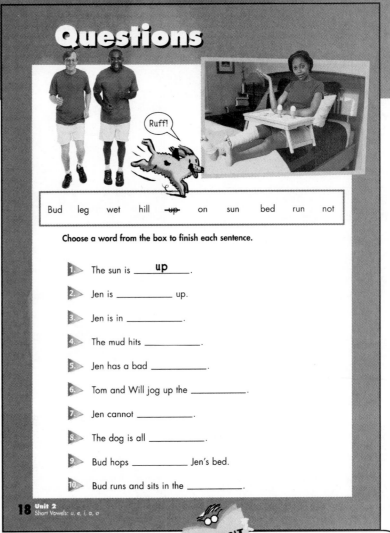

Questions

| Bud | leg | wet | hill | ~~up~~ | on | sun | bed | run | not |

Choose a word from the box to finish each sentence.

1. The sun is ___**up**___.

2. Jen is _____ up.

3. Jen is in _____.

4. The mud hits _____.

5. Jen has a bad _____.

6. Tom and Will jog up the _____.

7. Jen cannot _____.

8. The dog is all _____.

9. Bud hops _____ Jen's bed.

10. Bud runs and sits in the _____.

18 Unit 2
Short Vowels: u, e, i, a, o

Say It!

Let students work in pairs to check their answers by taking turns reading the sentences aloud. One partner recites his/her sentence and the listening partner identifies the word(s) with the short vowel sound. Then partners switch so the listening partner recites a sentence.

Write It!
Partner Dictation

After the partners correct answers together (above), have one partner be the "teacher" and dictate the completed sentences to the other partner. As you walk around during this activity, listen for correct pronunciations of the short vowels. Note: This activity also serves as an assessment. You may note which vowels are causing difficulty for students through their misspellings.

CONTENT LINKS

SCIENCE
/e/ /i/
Cells and Living Systems
Achieving Competence in Science by P. Cohen: Amsco School Publications, Inc., 1993

/e/
Exercise and Health
Content Points B by Johnston and Johnston: Addison Wesley Publishing Co., 1990

/e/ /i/ /a/
Chemistry: Elements and Matter
Earth and Physical Science by M. Christison and S. Bassano: Addison Wesley Publishing Co., 1992

/e/ /i/ /o/
Inventions: Thomas Edison
Skills Sharpener 3 by J. DeFilippo and C. Skidmore, Addison Wesley Publishing Co., 1994

Review

Short Vowels: a, o, i, u, e
New Words: Dad, Mom, Sis

Phonics Objectives

Can students:
- ✓ listen for and identify /a/, /o/, /i/, /u/, and /e/?
- ✓ read and write the letters for short vowels *a, o, i, u,* and *e* in words and sentences?

Language Acquisition Objectives

Students:
- read sentences and match them to pictures
- review the verbs *has, can, is, run*
- review plurals
- use words for family members: *Mom, Dad, Sis*

ESL Standards

- Goal 2, Standard 1

REVIEW a, o, i, u, e

Dad   Mom   Sis

Write the letter that matches the sentence.

1. Dad is on the hill. __b__

2. Mom has an egg. ____

3. Sis has a mitt. ____

4. A bug is in the box. ____

5. Jen cannot run. ____

6. Sis has lots of red pens. ____

7. A box is on the rug. ____

8. Dad is in the van. ____

Unit 2 **19**
Review of Short Vowels: u, e

FOCUSING ON PHONEMIC AWARENESS

Say the new words *Mom, Dad,* and *Sis.* Have students say these words together with you. Ask them what vowel sound they hear in each word. Make sure they pronounce the vowel in *Sis* as a short-*i* sound, not as a long-*e* (*Seese*). Sometimes students confuse these two sounds, especially speakers of romance languages like Spanish and French. Ask students to raise their hands when they hear a word that has the short-*i* as in *Sis.* You might say the following pairs of words: *meet/mitt, hill/heel, sit/seat, heat/hit.*

USING THE REVIEW PAGE

Ask students to:
- point to letters *a, o, i, u, e* that stand for /a/, /o/, /i/, /u/, /e/
- listen as you read words in box
- locate words as you repeat them
- read aloud and track words with you

BUILDING BACKGROUND

Ask students about the terms for family members in their own countries. Is there more than one word for *Mom*? Explain that English has several words for *Mom: mother, mama, ma, mommy,* etc. Is there more than one word for *Dad*? Again, English has many variations: *father, papa, pa, pop, daddy.* And *sister*? Explain that *Sis,* short for *sister,* rarely has other variations in English. Invite students who have a sister or sisters to raise their hands.

ACTIVITIES FOR ALL LEARNERS

Say It!
(Auditory Learners)

Ask students to brainstorm their own sentences using the family words: *Mom, Dad,* and *Sis.* List their ideas on the board. Encourage students to use expanded vocabulary for family members if they know more words.

Write It!

Divide the class into pairs or small groups. Have students write six sentences with the review verbs: *has, can, is, run.* Have them take turns reading the sentences aloud.

UNIT 2 Short Vowels: a, o, i, u, e   19

UNIT 3

Blends

Initial *l*-Blends: *cl, fl, pl, bl, gl, sl*

New Words: o'clock, flag, plant, black, glass, sled

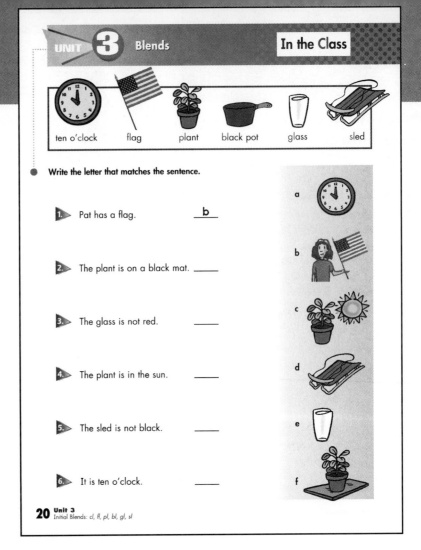

FOCUSING ON PHONEMIC AWARENESS

Pronounce the word *cap* for the class, stressing the /k/ sound. Next, say the word *lap*, stressing the /l/ sound. Say the word *clap* and model oral blending: *cllllaaaaap*. Pronounce the word *clap* more quickly and clap your hands. Ask students to do the same. Point out how the *cl* combines the sounds /k/ and /l/.

Remind students that the word *clap* is an imitation of the sound that two hands make when struck together.

Challenge the class to listen carefully as you say a list of words. If a word begins with the same consonant blend as *clap*, they should clap their hands. You may wish to use the following list of words: *cat, class, club, lab, can, cub, club*. You can repeat this activity with words using other initial *l*-blends, such as *fl, pl, bl, gl,* and *sl*.

USING THE PAGES

Page 20

Ask students to:
• point to the letters *cl, fl, pl, bl, gl, sl*
• locate words as you say them
• read aloud and track words with you

Read the title "In the Class" aloud and explain that in this lesson students will learn names for things that can be found in the classroom. Say the word *class*, stressing the initial *cl*. Have the students repeat the word after you. Then use the other words and illustrations in the box to point out the sound of *cl* as in *o'clock, fl* as in *flag, pl* as in *plant, bl* as in *black, gl* as in *glass,* and *sl* as in *sled*.

Telling Time: Point out the word *o'clock* in the box. Explain that the hour in English is expressed by the term *o'clock*. This tells the exact hour *of the clock*. Explain that the term *o'clock* is a contraction for the phrase *o(f the) clock*.

Page 21

Invite students to look over the illustration at the top of p. 21. Ask a volunteer to read aloud the sentence that is written on the chalkboard in the picture (*Bud is in the class.*).

Write *cl, fl, pl, bl, gl,* and *sl* on the chalkboard. Direct students' attention to the objects in the illustration which have names that begin with the letter combinations you have written. Point to each blend as you say the word (*class, clock, chalkboard, flag, plant, globe*). Challenge students to find things in their own classroom that begin with any of these blends. (*glue, glass, slot, slip of paper, plastic cup,* etc.)

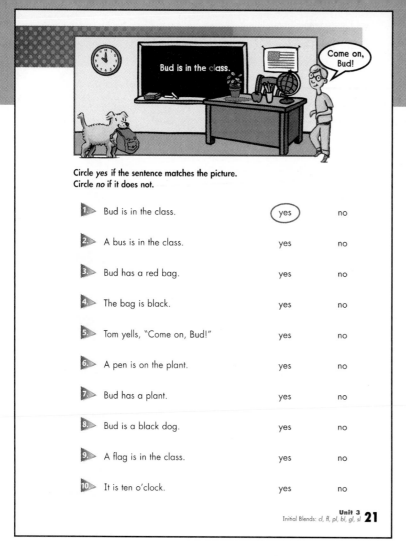

Circle *yes* if the sentence matches the picture.
Circle *no* if it does not.

1. Bud is in the class.   (yes)   no

2. A bus is in the class.   yes   no

3. Bud has a red bag.   yes   no

4. The bag is black.   yes   no

5. Tom yells, "Come on, Bud!"   yes   no

6. A pen is on the plant.   yes   no

7. Bud has a plant.   yes   no

8. Bud is a black dog.   yes   no

9. A flag is in the class.   yes   no

10. It is ten o'clock.   yes   no

Unit 3
Initial Blends: *cl, fl, pl, bl, gl, sl* **21**

ACTIVITIES FOR ALL LEARNERS

Set the Clock! (Telling Time in English)
(Kinesthetic Learners)

Materials: paper plates, metal brads, markers, tag board strips

Directions: You may wish to show students a finished paper-plate clock that you have made in advance as a sample. Explain that each person is going to: (1) mark numbers from 1 to 12 around the edge of his/her paper plate to create a clock face; (2) cut out clock hands from tag board strips; (3) punch holes in the ends of the clock hands with a paper punch; (4) attach the hands to the center of the paper-plate clock face with metal brads; (5) quiz a partner by setting the hands and asking, *What time is it now?*

Make Flags
(Visual Learners)

Materials: construction paper, glue, tape or stapler, string, scissors, markers

Directions: On the chalkboard, write the initial *l*-blend words *clock, flag, plant, black, glass,* and *sled.* Distribute the construction paper, glue, scissors, and markers. Ask students to draw a picture of their country's flag. Then ask them to cut the construction paper into the shape of a flag.

Place a long piece of string along a bulletin board or wall. Tape or staple the flag to the string. Have each student describe and explain the symbolism of his/her flag.

Extension Activity: You may wish to ask students to make a map of their country to display beside the flag.

Match the Sounds
(Auditory Learners)

Materials: index cards, markers

On large index cards, write the words *clock, flag, plant, glass,* and *sled.* Say each word aloud as you display it on the chalk rail. Invite the class to repeat it after you.

Next, say the word *plug* and ask a volunteer to lift up the index card that has the word that begins with the same sound. (*plant*) Repeat this activity with other words beginning with *cl, fl, pl, gl,* and *sl.* Some words you may use are *flip, flat, clap, club, glad, glow, sleep, slip, plum,* and *please.*

Sing a Short-*a* Song 🎧

🎵 Play the audiocassette of the song "You're a Grand Old Flag." Distribute copies of the lyrics on p. 95 and invite students to find the words which contain consonant blends. Have them circle those words. (*grand, flag, flying, emblem, free, brave, true, blue, brag*)

USING THE AUDIOCASSETTE 🎧

As you play the song again, invite students to sing along. Review the lyrics and be sure students understand the meaning of words like *high-flying, emblem, brave, boast, brag.* Ask if anyone knows the symbolism of the stars and stripes in the American flag (13 original colonies, 50 states). You may encourage students to research other aspects of early American history and report back to the class.

Write It!

✏️ Distribute writing paper to each student. One at a time, display picture cards of the initial *l*-blend words. Ask students to write the words for each picture. Review the work as a class. For added practice, you can display short vowel words from Units 1 and 2 and ask students to write those as well.

Initial *r*-Blends: *gr, fr, br, tr, cr, dr*

New Words: grass, frog, brick, pick-up truck, crab, dress

Phonics Objectives

Can students:
- ✓ listen for the sounds of initial *r*-blends *gr, fr, br, tr, cr,* and *dr*?
- ✓ identify the sounds the letter combinations *gr, fr, br, tr, cr,* and *dr* stand for?
- ✓ read and write initial *r*-blends in words and sentences?

Language Acquisition Objectives

Students:
- use words relating to the outdoors

ESL Standards

- Goal 1, Standard 1

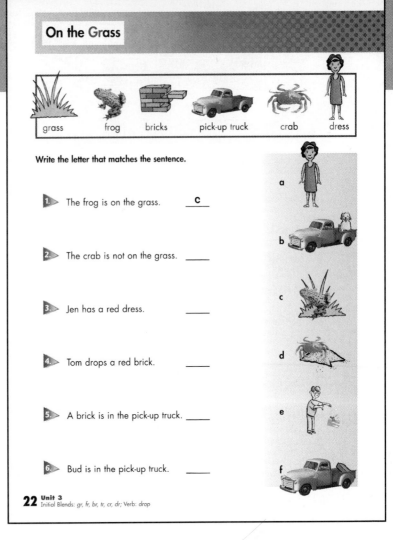

On the Grass

grass   frog   bricks   pick-up truck   crab   dress

Write the letter that matches the sentence.

1. The frog is on the grass.   c
2. The crab is not on the grass.   _____
3. Jen has a red dress.   _____
4. Tom drops a red brick.   _____
5. A brick is in the pick-up truck.   _____
6. Bud is in the pick-up truck.   _____

a
b
c
d
e
f

22 Unit 3
Initial Blends: gr, fr, br, tr, cr, dr; Verb: drop

FOCUSING ON PHONEMIC AWARENESS

Pronounce the word *grass* and model oral blending: *grrrraaaaass*. Ask the students to repeat the word *grass* after you. You may wish to ask a student to explain what grass is, or you can indicate the picture of grass at the top of p. 22. Point out how the initial *gr* combines the /g/ and /r/ sounds.

Challenge the class to listen carefully as you say a list of words. If a word contains a consonant sound blended with *r* (as in *grass*), they should raise their hand. You may wish to use the following list of words: *fog, frog, truck, tuck, cab, crab, brick, back, desk, dress*.

USING PAGE 22

Ask students to:
- point to the letters *gr, fr, br, tr, cr, dr*
- locate words as you say them
- read aloud and track words with you

Point out the picture of grass in the box. Show students how in the word *grass* the /g/ and /r/ sounds combine. Use the other words and illustrations in the box to introduce the initial *fr* as in *frog*, *br* as in *brick*, *tr* as in *truck*, *cr* as in *crab*, and *dr* as in *dress*.

ACTIVITIES FOR ALL LEARNERS

Rock, Plant, Grass
(Visual Learners)

Materials: picture cards of review words from Units 1, 2, and 3 (short vowels, *l*-blends, *r*-blends)

Directions: Divide the class into small groups. Explain that you are going to distribute picture cards of the words from Units 1, 2, and 3 to each group. Groups will have five minutes to find as many outdoor words as possible (*rock, plant, grass*). Any word which might be found both indoors and outdoors can count (*dog, clock*). The group with the most outdoor words wins.

Read It!

Play the audiocassette of p. 22. Have students (1) read along and listen to the following lines and (2) repeat them as directed. Check pronunciation of the sound *gr* carefully.

grass   frog   bricks
pick-up truck   crab   dress
1. The frog is on the grass.
2. The crab is not on the grass.
3. Jen has a red dress.
4. Tom drops a red brick.
5. A brick is in the pick-up truck.
6. Bud is in the pick-up truck.

Write It!

Distribute writing paper to each student. One at a time, display picture cards for the initial *r*-blend and *l*-blend words. Ask students to say the word for each picture and write the first two letters. Note: It is difficult for some students to distinguish between the sounds of *l* and *r* (*glass* and *grass*), and they may need more practice with these blends.

Initial s-Blends: st, sp, sn, sw, sk, sm

New Words: steps, spill, snack, swim, skin, smell

Phonics Objectives

Can students:
- ✓ listen for sounds of initial s-blends *st, sp, sn, sw, sk,* and *sm*?
- ✓ identify the sounds the letter combinations *st, sp, sn, sw, sk,* and *sm* stand for?
- ✓ read and write initial s-blends in words and sentences?

Language Acquisition Objectives

Can students:
- ✓ use the verbs *spill, swim, smell*?

ESL Standards

- Goal 1, Standard 2

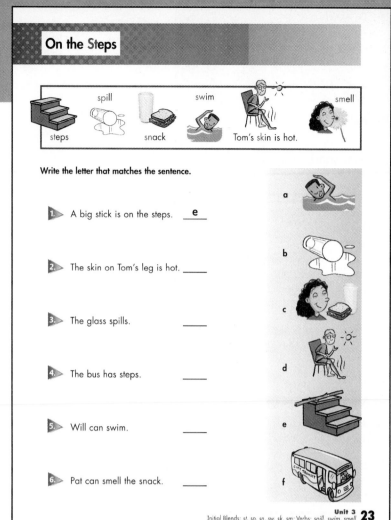

On the Steps

spill   swim   smell
steps   snack   Tom's skin is hot.

Write the letter that matches the sentence.

1. A big stick is on the steps. __e__

2. The skin on Tom's leg is hot. _____

3. The glass spills. _____

4. The bus has steps. _____

5. Will can swim. _____

6. Pat can smell the snack. _____

a
b
c
d
e
f

Unit 3 **23**
Initial Blends: *st, sp, sn, sw, sk, sm;* Verbs: *spill, swim, smell*

FOCUSING ON PHONEMIC AWARENESS

Say the word *sand*, stressing the initial /s/ sound. Next, say the word *Will*, stressing the /w/ sound. Say the word *swim* and model oral blending: *swwwiiiimmmm.* Invite students to say the word *swim.* Point out how the *sw* combines the /s/ and /w/ sounds.

Challenge the class to listen carefully as you say a list of words. If a word begins with the same sound as *swim*, they should raise their hands. You may wish to use the following list of words: *swan, swap, smell, sweet, spill, swat, snack.* You can repeat this activity with initial s-blends *st, sp, sn, sk,* and *sm.*

USING PAGE 23

Ask students to:
- point to the letters *st, sp, sn, sw, sk, sm*
- locate words as you say them
- read aloud and track words with you

Point to the picture of the steps on the page and say the word *steps*, stressing the initial *st*. Point out how the /s/ and /t/ sounds combine. Have the class repeat it. Use the other words and illustrations in the box to introduce the initial *sp* as in *spill, sn* as in *snack, sk* as in *skin*, and *sm* as in *smell.*

Song: "Swing Low, Sweet Chariot" (Auditory Learners) 🎧

Play the audiocassette of the song "Swing Low, Sweet Chariot." Distribute copies of the lyrics on p. 95 and invite students to find the words which contain *sw* consonant blends. Have them circle those words. (*swing, sweet*)

USING THE AUDIOCASSETTE 🎧

As you play the song again, invite students to sing along. Review the lyrics and be sure students understand the meaning of words like *chariot, Jordan* (River), *angels, heaven.* Explain the tradition of gospel music in the United States. Encourage stu-

dents to research other gospel tunes and play them for the class.

Say It!

Play a charades game by writing the words *steps, spill, swim, skin, smell, snack, grass, frog, brick, truck, crab,* and *dress* on slips of paper and placing them in a hat. Divide the class into teams and invite members of each team to act out a word that they pick from the hat for their team. Give points to teams that guess the right word.

Write It!

Ask students to listen carefully as you read a list of words. Instruct them to write down the first two letters of each word they hear. Use the following words, stressing the sounds of the initial s-blends: *snack* (*sn*), *spill* (*sp*), *step* (*st*), *swim* (*sw*), *smell* (*sm*), *skin* (*sk*), and *sled* (*sl*).

Final Blends: *nd, lk, mp, nk, ft*

New Words: sand, milk, jump, drink, gift

On the Sand

sand   Tom drinks his milk.   jump   gift

Write the word that finishes each sentence.

1. Bud runs on the ____**sand**____ .

2. A frog can _____ on a rock.

3. Jen has a glass of _____ .

4. Will has a _____ .

5. Tom _____ his milk.

6. Will can _____ .

24 Unit 3
Final Blends: *nd, lk, mp, nk, ft*; Verbs: *jump, drink, run, swim*

FOCUSING ON PHONEMIC AWARENESS

Pronounce the word *sand* for the class, stressing the final /nd/ sound. Next, pronounce the word *stand,* as you stand up. Point out how the final *nd* combines the sounds of the letters *n* and *d.* Have the students stand up and repeat the word *stand* with you.

Ask the class to listen as you say the following words and raise their hands if a word ends with the /nd/ sound: *band, spend,* jump, van, *land,* hat, *sand, send,* snack, *stand.* You can repeat this activity with final blends *lk, mp, nk,* and *ft.*

USING PAGE 24

Ask students to:
• point to letters *nd, lk, mp, nk, ft*
• locate words as you say them
• read aloud and track words with you

Point out the picture of the sand in the box. Explain how in the word *sand* the /n/

and the /d/ combine to make the *nd.* Invite the class to make the sound of *nd.* Use the other words and illustrations in the box to introduce the final *lk* as in *milk, mp* as in *jump, nk* as in *drink,* and *ft* as in *gift.*

ACTIVITIES FOR ALL LEARNERS

Blends Game: Concentration
(Kinesthetic/Visual Learners)

Materials: index cards, pen, scissors

Directions: Ask students for 20 words with blends and write their suggestions on the board. (Examples: *sand, milk, jump, drink, gift, snack, swim, smell, skin,* etc.) Have students choose partners. Distribute 30 index cards to each pair of students. Have them (1) cut the index cards in half and (2) write the first letters of each word on one-half of a card and the last letters on the other. (Example: MI/LK.) Ask students to mix up the cards and place them face down, then take turns flipping over two cards at a time. If the cards form a word, the student must say the word and

keep the card. If the cards don't form a word, he/she must turn the cards back over. The partner who has the most blend-words at the end of the game wins.

Say It!
Simon Says: Blends

Play Simon Says with the students. If they hear the action word with a final blend in the direction, they should say the word and do the action. If not, they should stay still. You can use directions like these: *Simon says: jump, run* (no blend), *drink, jog* (no blend), *sit* (no blend), *stand.* You may wish to invite a student to be "Simon" and lead the game with other verbs starting with blends.

Write It!

Ask the students to listen carefully as you read a list of 20 words with blends in them. Instruct them to write down the last two letters of each word they hear. (Examples: *drink, jump, milk, sand, gift, steps, spill, snack, swim, skin, smell,* etc.) Now ask them to write a sentence using each word.

Final Blends: *xt, st, sk, lp, lt, nt*

New Words: next, nest, desk, help, belt, tent

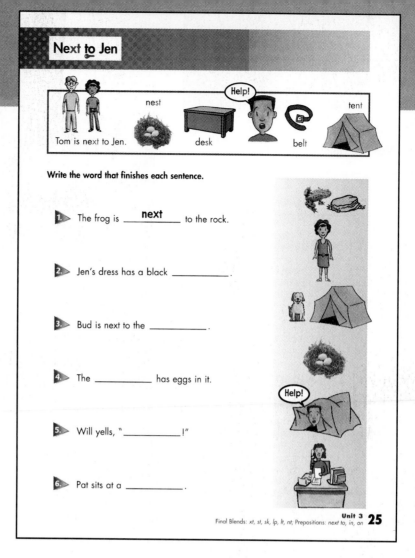

Next to Jen

Tom is next to Jen.   nest   desk   Help!   belt   tent

Write the word that finishes each sentence.

1. The frog is _____**next**_____ to the rock.

2. Jen's dress has a black _____.

3. Bud is next to the _____.

4. The _____ has eggs in it.

5. Will yells, "_____!"

6. Pat sits at a _____.

Final Blends: *xt, st, sk, lp, lt, nt*; Prepositions: *next to, in, on*   **Unit 3 25**

FOCUSING ON PHONEMIC AWARENESS

Make the /s/ sound. Have the class repeat it. Say the /k/ sound, having the class repeat it. Then point to a desk and say *desk*, focusing on the final *sk*. Say the word *desk* and model oral blending: *dessssk*. Invite the class to repeat it after you. Repeat this with the sounds in the other final blends: *xt* as in *next, st* as in *first, lp* as in *help, nt* as in *tent,* and *lt* as in *belt*.

USING PAGE 25

Ask students to:
• point to the letters *xt, st, sk, lp, lt, nt*
• locate words as you say them
• read aloud and track words with you

Point out the picture of Tom standing next to Jen in the box. Read *Tom is next to Jen* aloud. Point out how in the word *next*, the *x* and *t* together stand for the /kst/ sound.

Ask a student to say the word *next*, and then ask another student to say *next*. Continue until all the students have said *next*. Use the other words and illustrations in the box to introduce the final *st* as in *nest, sk* as in *desk, lp* as in *help, lt* as in *belt,* and *nt* as in *tent*.

ACTIVITIES FOR ALL LEARNERS

Read It!

Play the audiocassette of p. 25. Have students (1) read along and listen to the following lines and (2) repeat them as directed. Check pronunciation of the sound *xt* carefully.

Tom is next to Jen.
nest desk Help! belt tent
1. The frog is next to the rock.
2. Jen's dress has a black belt.
3. Bud is next to the tent.
4. The nest has eggs in it.
5. Will yells, "Help!"
6. Pat sits at a desk.

Say It!

Ask students to make double rows by pushing desks together side by side. Stand beside a student in one of the double rows and say, *I am next to (name of student beside you)*. Then ask that student to say, *I am next to (name of student beside him/her)*. Have students continue down the rows. Note: This activity can also be done with desks formed in a circle, with each student indicating the one next to him/her in the circle.

Write It!
Dictation

Ask the students to listen carefully for the blends as you read the following pairs of words: *frog/flag; next/nest; brick/black; desk/dress; swim/skin; belt/help*. Now ask the students to write each word as you reread the pairs slowly. Stress initial and final blends as you pronounce each word.

Initial /kw/ *qu*
New Words: quick, quiz

Quick Quiz

Circle *yes* if the question matches the picture.
Circle *no* if it does not.

1.	Is the gas pump next to the pick-up truck?	(yes)	no
2.	Is a man in the truck?	yes	no
3.	Is a man next to the truck?	yes	no
4.	Is a dog on the grass?	yes	no
5.	Is a fan belt on the grass?	yes	no
6.	Is Jen next to the truck?	yes	no
7.	Is a cat on the gas pump?	yes	no
8.	Is a desk in the truck?	yes	no
9.	Is a brick in the truck?	yes	no
10.	Is a van next to the gas pump?	yes	no

26 Unit 3
Blends

FOCUSING ON PHONEMIC AWARENESS

Pronounce the word *quick* for the class, stressing the *qu* sound. Ask students to repeat the word after you. Ask students what sound they hear at the beginning of the word. (/kw/) Let them repeat the sound. Challenge volunteers to model blending the sounds in the word *quick*. Point out how the sound is made up of /k/ and /w/ sounds that form the new /kw/ sound.

Ask students say raise their hands when they hear a word that begins with /kw/. Use the following words: *quick, quit, can, quilt, crab, queen, class,* and *quiz*.

USING PAGE 26

Read the title "Quick Quiz" aloud. Explain that *quick* is another word for *fast* and *quiz* is another word for *test*. Ask a volunteer to describe a true/false or yes/no quiz. Explain that some quizzes have questions to be answered and some have statements/sentences to be judged as true or false, yes or no. Ask students to look at the picture on the top of p. 26 and to name the objects. (*pick-up truck, fan belts, tree, grass, gas pump, bricks, girl next to the tree, cat, man*) Have a student read the example sentence and explain why *yes* is circled.

ACTIVITIES FOR ALL LEARNERS

Quick Things
(Visual Learners)

Materials: picture cards or magazines

Directions: Divide the class into three or four groups. Write the word *quick* on the chalkboard and pronounce it. Brainstorm things that are quick (cars, planes, rabbits, runners, etc.) Distribute picture cards or magazines to each group and ask them to make a list of the things they find that are quick. Have the groups share their lists and explain why they chose the items they did.

Say It!
He's Quick!

Play the audiocassette of the following chant:

Group 1: I have a friend.
Group 2: Who runs very fast.
Group 1: He's quick! (clap, clap)
Group 2: He's quick! (clap, clap)
Group 1: He's always first.
Group 2: He's never last.
Group 1: He's quick! (clap, clap)
Group 2: He's quick! (clap, clap)

Distribute copies of the chant on p. 95. Have students underline words containing the initial /kw/ sound.

Write It!
Write Your Own Quiz

Ask students to write a true/false quiz for a partner. Explain that the quiz should have 10 sentences in it. Some should be true and some false. You may wish to help them by writing a few sample sentences on the board, for example:

A truck is in the class. **True False**
A pen is on the desk. **True False**

New Words: truck, smell, o'clock, pants, belt, glass, milk, drop, spill, snack, steps, next to, grass, bricks, plants, sand, jump, stop

Phonics Objectives

Can students:
- ✓ listen for the sounds of initial and final blends?
- ✓ read initial and final blends in the context of a story?
- ✓ write words with initial and final blends?

Language Acquisition Objectives

Can students:
- ✓ read words in story context?
- ✓ use the verbs *drop, spill, jump, stop, get up, put on, run, has, is, jog*
- ✓ use the prepositions *in, on, next to*?

ESL Standards

- Goal 1, Standard 2

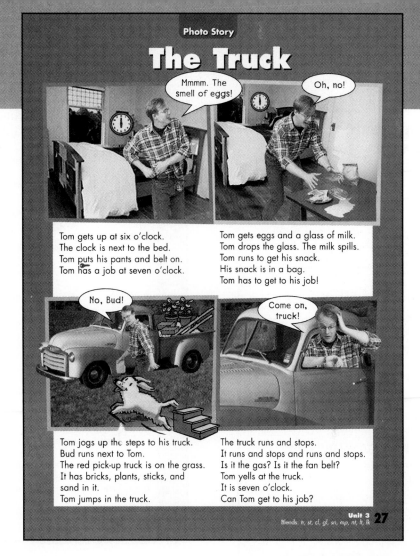

Photo Story

The Truck

Mmmm. The smell of eggs!

Oh, no!

Tom gets up at six o'clock.
The clock is next to the bed.
Tom puts his pants and belt on.
Tom has a job at seven o'clock.

Tom gets eggs and a glass of milk.
Tom drops the glass. The milk spills.
Tom runs to get his snack.
His snack is in a bag.
Tom has to get to his job!

No, Bud!

Come on, truck!

Tom jogs up the steps to his truck.
Bud runs next to Tom.
The red pick-up truck is on the grass.
It has bricks, plants, sticks, and sand in it.
Tom jumps in the truck.

The truck runs and stops.
It runs and stops and runs and stops.
Is it the gas? Is it the fan belt?
Tom yells at the truck.
It is seven o'clock.
Can Tom get to his job?

Unit 3 27
Blends: *tr, st, cl, gl, sn, mp, nt, lt, lk*

FOCUSING ON PHONEMIC AWARENESS

Song: "The Pick-up Truck" 🎧
(Auditory Learners)

 Teach the class the following song. Ask students to listen for the blends.

Poor old Tom is out of luck
He's got a problem with his
  pick-up truck
He's got a job at seven o'clock
But his truck just runs and stops.
He steps off the truck
Stands next to the back
He looks at the sand and the
  bricks and the sticks.
He jumps back in and yells at
  the truck.
It's seven o'clock and Tom is
  out of luck.
Hey! Can you move that truck?

USING THE AUDIOCASSETTE 🎧

Play the audiocassette of the song again. Distribute copies of the lyrics on p. 95. Have them circle the words that have blends in them. (*truck, sand, stop, jump*)

USING THE PHOTO STORY

🎧 **Preview** the photo story "The Truck" with your students. Ask students to follow along as you play the audiocassette of the story. Students may wish to track the words as the story is read.

Background discussion: Ask the students if they have a job. Ask them if they have ever had problems getting to their job on time. Encourage them to relate their own personal experiences. Prompt them with additional questions about their work.

Read the photo story together. You may wish to assign volunteers to read the part of Tom and the four narrators—one reader for each set of caption lines under the four pictures. As students read, listen for correct pronunciation of the consonant blends in the New Words (above). Discuss problem words and errors in pronunciation after the reading. Model the correct pronunciations for students and ask them to repeat the words after you.

Review the story. Lead the class in a second reading of "The Truck." This time, ask for new volunteers to read aloud. After they finish reading, ask questions focusing on the content of the story:

- Who gets up at six o'clock? (*Tom*)
- What does he smell? (*eggs*)
- What does Tom put on? (*his pants and belt*)
- What does he drop? (*a glass of milk*)
- Where does he have to go? (*to his job*)
- Who runs next to Tom? (*Bud*)
- What is in the pick-up truck? (*bricks, plants, sticks, and sand*)
- What does Tom say to his truck when it runs and stops? (*"Come on, truck!"*)

Initial Blends: *tr, dr, gr, br, sm, sp, sn, st, cl, gl, pl*
Final Blends: *nt, nd, lt, lk, xt, mp,*

New Words: truck, smell, o'clock, pants, belt, glass, milk, drop, spill, snack, steps, next to, grass, bricks, plants, sand, jump, stop

Phonics Objectives

Can students:

✓ listen for initial and final blends?
✓ identify the sounds of consonant blends *tr, dr, gr, br, sm, sp, sn, st, cl, gl, pl, nt, nd, lt, lk, xt, mp*?
✓ read and write letters for initial and final blends in words and sentences?

Language Acquisition Objectives

Students:

• review verbs *drop, spill, jump, stop, get up, put on, run, has, is, jog*
• review prepositions *in, at, next to*
• use words related to daily routines (*getting up, getting dressed, eating*)
• read and comprehend familiar words in a new context

ESL Standards

• Goal 2, Standard 1

BUILDING BACKGROUND

Ask students what is happening in the picture at the top of p. 28. Ask students to talk about what Tom is doing. Can they retell what happened in the story on the previous page without turning back to look? Invite students to talk about different things they do to get ready in the morning. Review the events of the photo story together.

Questions

Number the sentences 1–10 in the order they happened in the story.

1. ▷ Tom jumps in his truck. _____
2. ▷ The truck runs and stops. _____
3. ▷ Tom gets up at six o'clock. ___1___
4. ▷ It is 7:00 and Tom cannot get to his job. _____
5. ▷ Tom puts his pants and belt on. _____
6. ▷ Tom yells, "Come on, truck!" _____
7. ▷ Tom jogs up the steps. _____
8. ▷ Tom gets eggs and a glass of milk. _____
9. ▷ The truck is on the grass. _____
10. ▷ Tom runs to get his snack. _____

28 Unit 3
Blends

USING PAGE 28

Read the instructions at the top of p. 28 to the students. Review what is happening in the picture. Explain that the sentences on this page need to be placed in the order that they happened in the story. Ask a student to read sentence 3 which has a *1* by it. Suggest that students read each sentence and try to find the one that tells what happened second in the story (5. *Tom puts his pants and belt on.*). They should write *2* by this sentence. Ask the students to try to remember the events in the story and finish numbering the sentences in order from 1 to 10. If they need to check an answer, they can turn back and reread p. 27.

CONTENT LINKS

Social Studies/U.S. Government

/st/ /br/ /nt/ /gr/ /pr/ /cr/ /bl/
The Constitution of the United States; Branches of the U.S. Government; Congress: The House of Representatives; The Supreme Court; Democracy
S.T.A.R. Social Studies by M. Cristison and S. Bassano: Addison Wesley Publishing Co., 1993

/st/ /nt/
The Federal System of Government
Content Points B by Johnston and Johnston: Addison Wesley Publishing Co., 1990

/fr/
Basic Freedoms: The Bill of Rights
Skills Sharpener 4 by J. DeFilippo and C. Skidmore: Addison Wesley Publishing Co., 1994

Review

Blends and Short Vowels

New Words: dog, desk, grass, class, bus, run, pens, dress, hit, sit

---

~~dog~~	grass	bus	pens	hit
desk	class	run	dress	sits

Self Test: Write the word that finishes each sentence.

1. Bud is a big ____dog____ .

2. Will can _____ the ball.

3. Bud and Tom can _____ .

4. Pat and Tom get on the _____ .

5. Jen has ten red _____ .

6. A frog hops in the _____ .

7. A plant is on the _____ .

8. A flag is in the _____ .

9. Will _____ on a hill.

10. Jen has a red _____ .

FOCUSING ON PHONEMIC AWARENESS

To practice the initial and final blends introduced in Unit 3, ask students to repeat a series of action words using those blends. As they repeat each word after you, invite the class to mime the action suggested by the word. Use the following words: *jump, clap, step, swim, smell, drink, drop, stop.*

USING THE REVIEW PAGE

Ask students to:

• point to the letters *sk, gr, mp, dr*
• locate words as you say them
• read aloud and track words with you

Ask the class to look at the words in the box at the top of the page. Ask for volunteers to read each word aloud. You may want to point out the words that contain blends: *grass, desk, jump,* and *dress*. Tell the class that they are going to use those words to complete sentences on the page.

ACTIVITIES FOR ALL LEARNERS

Make a Blend Poster
(Visual Learners)

Materials: newspapers, catalogs, magazines, scissors, construction paper, glue, markers

Directions: Divide the class into pairs or small groups. Distribute the materials. Ask each group to look for pictures of objects whose names start with the blends taught in this unit (*green grass, dress, truck, skirt,* etc.). When the groups have cut out their pictures, ask them to glue the pictures onto poster paper, making a collage of blends. Have them share their poster with the class, naming each object.

Say It!
Verb–Card Pantomime

 Shuffle index cards with the words *jump, hit, sit, step, stop, clap, spill, drop, drink, swim,* and *smell* written on them. Then ask a volunteer to come to

the front of the class. Ask the student to read a card without showing it to the other students. Ask him/her to act out the action written on the card and challenge the other students to guess and say the word that is written on the card. The student who first guesses correctly gets to pick the next card and act out the word.

Write It!
Blends in the News

 Materials: newspapers, pens, paper

Directions: Distribute newspapers to each student. Ask the students to circle the words they find in the newspaper which have blends in them. (Examples: *Congress, state, president, trucks, sports,* etc.) Ask students to copy the sentence or phrase from the newspaper which contains the blend-word they have circled. They should try to find and write twenty sentences or phrases that contain blends.

UNIT 4

Long Vowels: a

Long Vowels: /ā/ a–e

New Words: make, cake, take, plate, wake, wave, lake, snake, grapes

---

Phonics Objectives

Can students:
- ✓ listen for the long-*a* sound?
- ✓ identify the long-*a* sound formed by the letter combination *a–e*?
- ✓ read and write words and sentences with the long-*a* (*a–e*) sound?

Language Acquisition Objectives

Students:
- use the verbs *make, take, wake*

ESL Standards

- Goal 2, Standard 2

Focusing on Phonemic Awareness

Say the word *snack* and write it on the board. Explain that vowels can have more than one sound in English. Now say *snake* and model oral blending: *snaaaaake*. Write *snake* on the board, underlining the *a* and silent *e*. Indicate the snake picture at the top of p. 30.

Using Page 30

Ask students to:
- point to the letters *a–e*
- locate words as you say them
- read aloud and track words with you

Read the sentence *May makes a cake.* Write *makes* and *cake* on the board. Ask a student to read the other sentences in the box. Discuss the meaning of each new word. Point out the vowel–consonant–vowel (VCV) patterns in each long-*a* word.

Activities for All Learners

Take the Cake!
(Visual Learners)

Materials: paper, pens, a cake cut into small pieces (or a picture of a cake cut into pieces), picture cards, a large manila envelope

Directions: Divide the class into pairs. Explain that partners should write the word for the picture that you show. When they have 10 correct words, that pair can "take the cake." Draw the cards out of a large manila envelope one at a time. If there is a caption on the card, be sure that it is covered or kept below the opening of the envelope. Draw cards until everyone has had a chance to "take the cake."

Read It! 🎧

Play the audiocassette of p. 30. Have students (1) and listen to the following lines and (2) repeat them as

directed. Check pronunciation of the sound long-*a* carefully.

> May makes a cake.
> May takes a plate.
> May wakes up.
> waves in a lake   snake and grapes

1. May makes a cake.
2. May wakes up at six o'clock.
3. May's plate has grapes on it.
4. The lake has waves.
5. The snake is not in the lake.
6. May takes a glass of milk.

Write It!

✎ Write the words *lake, snake, plate, cake, grapes,* and *wake* on the chalkboard. Read the following riddles to the class and have students write down the long-*a* word answer.

- You can put food on me. (*plate*)
- You do this every morning. (*wake*)
- You can swim in me. (*lake*)
- I'm an animal with no legs. (*snake*)
- This is a small, purple fruit. (*grapes*)
- You get this on your birthday. (*cake*)

Long Vowels: /ā/ ay

New Words: play, gray, day, say, lay, tray, table

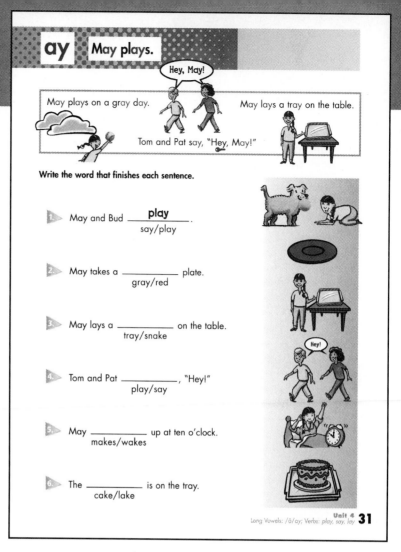

Phonics Objectives

Can students:
- ✓ listen for the long-*a* sound?
- ✓ identify the long-*a* sound formed by the letter combination *ay*?
- ✓ read and write words and sentences with the long-*a* (*ay*) sound?

Language Acquisition Objectives

Can students:
- ✓ use the verbs *play, say, lay*?

ESL Standards

- Goal 2, Standard 2

FOCUSING ON PHONEMIC AWARENESS

Show picture cards of long-*a* words, such as *grapes, plate, table, tray,* and *snake.* Repeat the words together. Now tell the class you are going to name pairs of words. Ask them to raise their hands if both words in the pair have the long-*a* sound. Use the following words: *day/pay, big/bag, stay/away, bad/sad, say/tray, play/gray, hit/hat, grass/glass, plate/lake.*

USING PAGE 31

Ask students to:
- point to the letters *ay*
- locate words as you say them
- read aloud and track words with you

Point out the title of the page—"May plays"—and read it aloud. Explain that the long-*a* sound is formed in a new way in this sentence. (*ay*) Ask a volunteer to read the first sentence in the box aloud, then find the words with the long-*a* sound. Do

the same with the other two sentences. Make sure students understand the meaning of each sentence.

ACTIVITIES FOR ALL LEARNERS

Plays/Movies/Dramas
(Kinesthetic/Auditory Learners)

Ask the students what plays or movies they have seen lately. Explain that the noun *play* in English refers to a live stage production. Divide the class into small groups and challenge them to make up a short play called "The Gray Day." Invite the groups to perform their short play for the rest of the class.

Say It!

Play the audiocassette of the following chant:

Group 1: It's such a gray (clap, clap) gray day. (clap, clap)
Group 2: We have to stay (clap, clap) inside today. (clap, clap)

Group 1: Inside the house (clap, clap) on this gray day (clap, clap)
Group 2: This is no fun (clap, clap), NO WAY! (clap, clap)

Distribute copies of the chant on p. 96. Have students underline words containing the long-*a* sound. Divide the class in two groups and repeat the chant together.

Write It!

Ask students to fold a piece of paper vertically, making two columns. Have them write *day* on the top of one column and *cake* on the top of the other. Explain that you are going to read a list of words. If the word has the long-*a* sound represented by the letters *ay*, students should list it under *day*. If the word has the long-*a* sound represented by the letters *a–e*, they should list it in the column under *cake*. Use the following words: *play, plate, say, make, lake, wave, lay, snake, grapes, May, gray, wake, tray, game.*

Long Vowels: /ā/ ai

New Words: wait, rain, hail, snail, pail, mail box, train, great

Phonics Objectives

Can students:
- ✓ listen for the long-*a* sound?
- ✓ identify the long-*a* sound formed by the letter combination *ai*?
- ✓ read and write words and sentences with the long-*a* (*ai*) sound?

Language Acquisition Objectives

Can students:
- ✓ use the verb *wait*?
- ✓ use words relating to the weather?

ESL Standards

- Goal 2, Standard 2

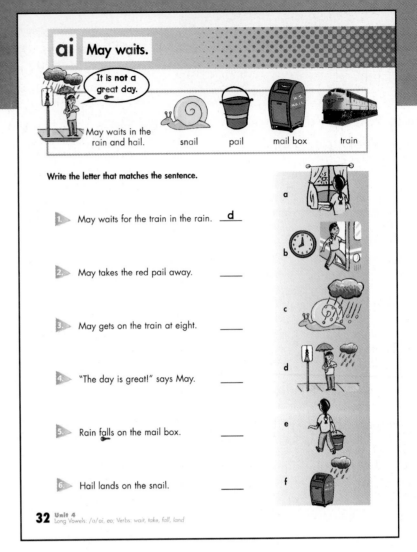

Write the letter that matches the sentence.

1. May waits for the train in the rain. __d__
2. May takes the red pail away. ____
3. May gets on the train at eight. ____
4. "The day is great!" says May. ____
5. Rain falls on the mail box. ____
6. Hail lands on the snail. ____

BUILDING BACKGROUND

Say the words *wave* and *play*, and model oral blending: *wwaaave, plaaaay.* Ask, *What do both words have in common?* (long-*a* sound) On the board, write the two words. Ask a volunteer to circle the letters in each word that stand for the long-*a* sound. (*a* and *e* in *wave*; *ay* in *play*)

Tell students that there is a third way to make the long-*a* sound. Write the word *train* on the chalkboard. Say the word stressing the long-*a* sound (*traaaiin*). Underline the letters *ai* in *train*. Explain that these letters also stand for the long-*a* sound. Point to the key icon under the word *great*. Explain that sometimes the letters *ea* also make a long-*a* sound.

USING PAGE 32

Ask students to:
- point to the letters *ai*
- locate words as you say them
- read aloud and track words with you

Read aloud the sentence May waits in the rain and hail. Explain that the long-a sound is formed here in two different ways. (ay, ai) Ask a student to tell you which words have the long-a sound.

ACTIVITIES FOR ALL LEARNERS

You've Got Mail
(Kinesthetic/Visual Learners)

Ask students if they have used e-mail. Explain that e-mail means electronic (or computer) mail. If possible, arrange to take students to a computer lab, where an experienced computer user can demonstrate e-mail. Have students set up e-mail accounts on one of the free e-mail sites. Invite them to share e-mail addresses and send each other e-mail messages. You might also send them individual e-mail messages.

Say It!

Play the audiocassette of the following chant:

Group 1: No need to wait. You have e-mail.
Group 2: You've got mail. You've got mail.
Group 1: It's never late in rain or hail.
Group 2: You've got mail. You've got mail.
Group 1: This is great! It cannot fail!
Group 2: You've got mail. You've got mail.

Distribute copies of the chant on p. 96. Have students underline words containing the long-*a* sound. Divide the class in two groups and repeat the chant together.

Write It!

Ask students to reread the sentences on p. 32 and underline the words which have the long-*a* sound. Have them make a list of these words and write eight new sentences using the words.

Long Vowels: /ā/ *ace, age*

New Words: face, page, race, cage, stage

Phonics Objectives

Can students:
- ✓ listen for the long-*a* + soft-*c* and long-*a* + soft-*g* sounds?
- ✓ identify the long-*a* + soft-*c* sounds formed by *ace* and the long-*a* + soft-*g* sounds formed by *age*?
- ✓ read and write words and sentences with the long-*a* + soft-*c* and long-*a* + soft-*g* sounds?

Language Acquisition Objectives

Can students:
- ✓ use the verb *have*?

ESL Standards

- Goal 2, Standard 1

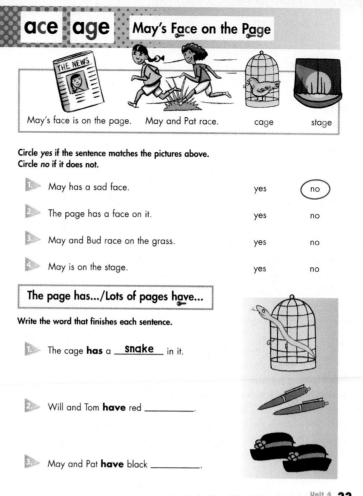

ace | age — May's Face on the Page

May's face is on the page.   May and Pat race.   cage   stage

Circle *yes* if the sentence matches the pictures above.
Circle *no* if it does not.

1. May has a sad face.   yes   (no)
2. The page has a face on it.   yes   no
3. May and Bud race on the grass.   yes   no
4. May is on the stage.   yes   no

The page has.../Lots of pages have...

Write the word that finishes each sentence.

1. The cage **has** a __snake__ in it.
2. Will and Tom **have** red _____.
3. May and Pat **have** black _____.

Long Vowels: /ā/ *a-e*; /k/ *c*, /s/ *c*, /g/ *g*, /j/ *g*; Verbs: *have, has*   **Unit 4 33**

FOCUSING ON PHONEMIC AWARENESS

Explain that the letters *g* and *c* have more than one sound in English. Remind students that they have already learned the hard /g/ sound of *g* as in *bag*. Explain that when the letter *g* appears between an *a* and an *e*, it often makes the /j/ sound or soft-*g* sound.

Next, write the word *face* on the board and invite the class to repeat it after you. Ask a student to point to his/her face. Explain that when the letter *c* appears between an *a* and an *e* it usually makes the /s/ sound in English.

USING PAGE 33

Ask students to:
- point to the letters *ace, age*
- locate the words that contain these letters
- read aloud and track words with you

Say the words *face* and *cage*. What are the two different sounds the letter *c*

makes in these words? (/s/, /k/) Then say the words *page* and *grass*. What are the two different sounds the letter *g* makes in these words? (/j/, /g/)

Ask students to look at the word *have* on the bottom half of the page. Explain that *have* is the plural form of the verb *has*. It is used for plural subjects, for example, *Will and Tom **have** red pens* (sentence 2).

ACTIVITIES FOR ALL LEARNERS

Faces on the Page

Materials: newspapers, magazines, scissors, glue, poster paper

Directions: Have students choose partners. Distribute materials and explain that students are to find interesting faces in the newspapers and magazines, cut them out, and glue them on the poster paper to make a collage. Encourage artistic arrangements and abstract compositions. Students can cut out partial faces or glue sections of unlike faces together to create Picasso-like collages.

Read It!

Play the audiocassette of p. 33. Have students (1) read along and listen to the following lines and (2) repeat them as directed. Check pronunciation of the long-*a* words that contain soft-*g* and soft-*c*.

May's face is on the page.
May and Pat race.
cage   stage
1. May has a sad face.   no
2. The page has a face on it.   yes
3. May and Bud race on the grass.   no
4. May is on the stage.   no

The page has . . . /Lots of pages have . . .
1. The cage has a snake in it.
2. Will and Tom have red pens.
3. May and Pat have black hats.

Write It!

Ask students to write 20 sentences using long-*a* words. Some sentences should have soft-*c* and soft-*g* words in them (*cage, page, face, race*).

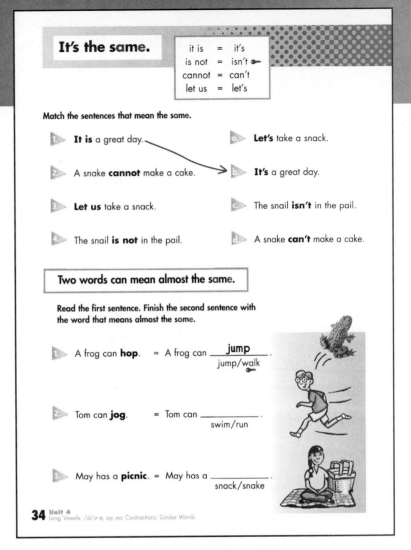

It's the same.

it is	=	it's
is not	=	isn't
cannot	=	can't
let us	=	let's

Match the sentences that mean the same.

1. **It is** a great day.

2. A snake **cannot** make a cake.

3. **Let us** take a snack.

4. The snail **is not** in the pail.

6. **Let's** take a snack.

5. **It's** a great day.

7. The snail **isn't** in the pail.

8. A snake **can't** make a cake.

Two words can mean almost the same.

Read the first sentence. Finish the second sentence with the word that means almost the same.

1. A frog can **hop**. = A frog can ___**jump**___ .
   jump/walk

2. Tom can **jog**. = Tom can _____ .
   swim/run

3. May has a **picnic**. = May has a _____ .
   snack/snake

34 Unit 4
Long Vowels: /ā/a-e, ay, ea; Contractions; Similar Words

Phonics Objectives

Can students:
- ✓ listen for the long-*a* sound?
- ✓ identify the long-*a* sound formed by different letter combinations?
- ✓ read and write words and sentences with the long-*a* sound?

Language Acquisition Objectives

Can students:
- ✓ use the contractions *it's, isn't, can't, let's*?
- ✓ use similar words?

ESL Standards

- Goal 1, Standard 1

BUILDING BACKGROUND

Write the sentence *It is cold!* on the board and read it aloud. Next, write *It's cold!* Explain that *it's* means the same thing as *it is*. Explain that a contraction is a short way of writing two words as one. Explain that the verb *contract* means *to make smaller or shrink*. On the board, write *it is* and then erase the letter *i* in *is* and substitute an apostrophe. Invite students to come to the board and do more examples by erasing letters to make contractions. (Examples: *cannot = can't, let us = let's, is not = isn't*.)

USING PAGE 34

Ask students to:
- locate words as you say them
- read aloud and track words with you

Review the first contraction in the box. Explain that *it's* means the same as *it is*. Have students look at the second line. Say the word *isn't* and explain that it means

the same as *is not*. Explain the contractions *can't* and *let's*.

ACTIVITIES FOR ALL LEARNERS

Concentration
(Kinesthetic/Visual Learners)

Materials: index cards, pens

Directions: Students will match groups of words with their corresponding contractions or synonyms. (1) On some of the index cards, write the following: *it is, is not, cannot,* and *let us*. On other cards write the contractions: *it's, isn't, can't, let's*. (2) On other sets of cards write synonym pairs (*hop/jump, jog/run, snack/picnic, sad/not happy, race/run, fall/drop*). Mix up the cards and place them face down. Invite students to play the game with a partner. Players turn over two cards at a time. If the cards have matching contractions or synonyms, the player can keep both cards. If the cards do not match, the player must turn them back over, remembering their location. The player with the most matching pairs wins.

Say It!

Play the audiocassette of the following chant:

Group 1: Is it big?
Group 2: No, it's not.
Group 1: Let's see. What can it be? Can it run?
Group 2: No, it can't.
Group 1: Let's see. What can it be? Is it a pan? Is it a pot?
Group 2: No, it isn't. No, it's not.

Distribute copies of the chant on p. 96. Have students circle the contractions. Divide the class in two groups and repeat the chant together.

Write It!

Dictate the following sentences:

1. It is six o'clock.
2. The man is not in the bus.
3. Tom cannot jump up.
4. Let us play ball.

Ask students to recopy each sentence, this time substituting contractions for *It is, is not, cannot, Let us*.

Photo Play: "A Day at the Lake"

New Words: May, day, lake, great, wake, eight, take, today, make, grapes, cake, plate, okay, lay, wait, snail, gray, waves, play, snake, rain, let's, can't

Phonics Objectives

Can students:
- ✓ listen for the short vowel and long-*a* sounds?
- ✓ read short vowel and long-*a* words in the context of a story?
- ✓ write words with long-*a*?

Language Acquisition Objectives

Can students:
- ✓ read words in a story context?
- ✓ use verbs and contractions?

ESL Standards

- Goal 1, Standard 2

A Day at the Lake

Names in the play: May, Pat, Will, Tom, Narrator

Narrator: The sun is up. It's a great day. May calls Pat.

May: Hey, wake up, Pat! It's eight o'clock.

Pat: Is it eight?

May: Yes, get up! Let's have a picnic at the lake.

Pat: Great! Let's call Will, Jen, and Tom.

May: And Bud! Let's take the dog.

Pat: Tom can take the truck.

May: Tom can't take the truck. It stops.

Pat: Okay. Let's take the van.

Narrator: Will sits on the steps. May calls Will.

May: Hey, Will! Let's have a picnic at the lake today.

Will: Great! Can Pat take the van?

May: Yes. But Tom can't take his truck.

Will: Can Jen make a snack?

May: Yes. Jen has the snack and the drinks. Tom and Pat have the grapes and the cake.

Will: Wait. Can Jen get the plates?

May: Pat has the plates in the van.

Will: Okay.

Unit 4 Long Vowels: a͞e, o͝y, o͞i **35**

FOCUSING ON PHONEMIC AWARENESS

Song: "A Day at the Lake" 🎧

 Play the audiocassette of the following song:

May tells Pat, "Let's have a picnic at the lake."
Pat says, "Great!"
Tom can't take the truck so they take the van.
That's okay.
Snacks and drinks and grapes and cakes and waves in the lake.
Look at Bud. What's this? Look at Bud. Has he got a snake?
No, it's a stick! Let's take a break!
They play all day and then the sky turns gray.
A day at the lake then comes to an end.
It looks like rain. Can't wait to do it again!

Distribute copies of the song on p. 96. Have students underline words containing the long-*a* sounds.

USING THE PHOTO PLAY

🎧 **Preview** the photo play "A Day at the Lake" with your students. Allow the students time to look through the play and examine the pictures and text. Ask students to read along as they listen to the audiocassette of the play.

Background discussion: Ask the students if they have ever taken a picnic to the beach. Have they ever been to a lake? Was it a sunny day? Have they ever been caught in the rain during a picnic? Encourage them to relate their own personal experiences. Prompt them with additional questions about their outings. Do they like playing games on the beach? Have they ever seen a snake?

Read the photo play together. Assign volunteers to read the parts of May, Pat, Will, Tom, and the narrator. As students read their parts, listen for correct pronunciation of the long-*a* sound. Do not interrupt the dialogue, but discuss problem words and errors in pronunciation after the reading. Model the correct pronunciations for students and ask them to repeat the words after you.

Review the events that happen in the play. Lead the class in a second reading of "A Day at the Lake." This time, ask for new volunteers to read the parts. After they finish reading, ask questions focusing on the action in the play.

- Who calls Pat? (*May*)
- What does May say? ("*Wake up! It's eight o'clock.*")
- What does May want to do? (*have a picnic at the lake*)
- Who does May call next? (*Will*)
- Can Pat take the van? (*yes*)
- Who can make the snack? (*Jen*)
- What is on the plate? (*grapes and a snail*)
- What does Bud find? (*a snake*)

ACTIVITIES FOR ALL LEARNERS

Act Out the Play "A Day at the Lake"
(Kinesthetic/Auditory Learners)

Materials: two telephones, a picnic blanket, a picnic basket, a ball, paper plates, grapes, a snail shell, a stick, a rubber snake (note: props can be made of paper)

Directions: Ask for volunteers to act out the play "A Day at the Lake." Assign the roles of May, Pat, Will, Tom, the narrator, Bud (the dog), and a prop person. Have the prop person set up: (1) two chairs for the phone conversation scene—stage left, and (2) a beach scene with the blanket, paper plates, food, etc.—stage right. Students can act out the story as they read the play or they can memorize their parts in advance. You may wish to assign a prompter in the latter case to help those who forget their lines. Practice the play several times, then perform it for a different class. You may wish to perform the play more than once, perhaps with a new cast.

Say it!
Beach Games

Ask students to look carefully at the photo of May and Tom at the bottom of p. 36. What beach game might they be playing (volleyball, catch, keep-away)? Could they be playing soccer? Why or why not? Ask students what games they play when they go to the beach. Do they play any water games? Do girls and boys play the games together? You may wish to take this opportunity to discuss different customs for outdoor activities in different countries.

Write It!
Long-*a* Words in the Play

Ask students to fold a piece of notebook paper into six columns (in half vertically, then in thirds vertically again). Have them write their name across the top of the paper. Next, at the top of each column, ask the students to write the name of a character in the play "A Day at the Lake." They can check the five charac-

ters in the play at the top of p. 35. (The sixth folded column may be left blank.) Explain that they should write all the long-*a* words that each character says under that person's name. As an example, you can write *Narrator* on the board with the words *great, day, May, grapes, cake*, etc., listed under it. Students may work in pairs if they wish, but each must complete his/her own written paper with lists of long-*a* words under the names of the different characters. Have students share their papers and compare answers. How many different long-*a* words are in this play?

Narrator: *Jen makes a snack of grapes and cake. At the lake, May lays the picnic on the sand.*

Tom: Wait, May! A snail is on the plate.

May: It's not a snail. It's a big grape.

Tom: No, it's not. It's a snail!

Will: Come on. The snail can wait. Let's swim.

May: No. The lake has gray waves.

Pat: Let's walk next to the lake.

Tom: No. Let's play ball.

May and Pat: Okay. Great!

Narrator: *Tom, May, and Pat play a ball game. Bud takes a stick and runs in the waves. But is it a stick?*

May: Hey, get the dog! Bud has a stick!

Tom: Is it a stick?

Pat: No, it's a snake!

Tom: Bud, drop the snake!

Pat: Drop the snake, Bud!

Tom: Jump on it, Pat.

Pat: No. It's big!

Narrator: *The snake gets away. Bud runs on the sand. The day gets gray. Rain falls on the picnic. Jen, Pat, Tom, and Will run to the van.*

May: It is *not* a great day!

36 Unit 4
Long Vowels: a–e, ay, ai

CONTENT LINKS

LITERATURE
/ā/ a–e
Tales of Courage, Tales of Dreams by John Mundahl: Addison Wesley Publishing Co., 1993

Tales from Many Cultures by Penny Cameron: Addison Wesley Publishing Co., 1995

Short Takes in Fiction by Robert L. Saltz and Francine B. Stieglitz: Addison Wesley Publishing Co., 1993

/ā/ a–e, /ā/ ay
Folk Tale Plays by Paul T. Nolan: Plays Inc., 1982

/ā/ ay
Power Play: Individuals in Conflict by Brenda Dyer: Prentice-Hall, 1996

/ā/ ea
Great American Short Stories by C. G. Draper: Pearson Education, 2001

Questions

New Words: May, lake, grapes, cake, plate, waves, race, face, gray, snail, rain, play, snake

Phonics Objectives

Can students:
- ✓ listen for the long-*a* sound?
- ✓ identify the long-*a* sound formed by different letter combinations?
- ✓ read and write words with the long-*a* and consonant blend sounds?
- ✓ listen for the /s/ *c* and /j/ *g* in words and read words containing them?

Language Acquisition Objectives

Students:
- use verbs
- use prepositions

ESL Standards

- Goal 1, Standard 3

Questions

Circle *yes* if the sentence matches the picture.
Circle *no* if it does not.

1. May, Tom, and Pat play a game on the sand. (yes) no
2. Rain lands on the grapes. yes no
3. Tom swims in the waves. yes no
4. A snail is on the plate. yes no
5. Pat and Tom have a race. yes no
6. The cake is next to the grapes. yes no
7. May's face is sad. yes no
8. The lake is gray. yes no
9. Tom has a snake. yes no
10. Bud has a stick. yes no

FOCUSING ON PHONEMIC AWARENESS

Remind the students that the long-*a* sound can be formed by many different letter combinations. Say the words *May, snake,* and *rain.* Ask the students to repeat the words after you. What letters form the long-*a* sound in *May*? (*ay*) What letters form the long-*a* sound in *snake*? (*a–e*) What letters form the long-*a* sound in *rain*? (*ai*) Ask a student to name something or someone in the classroom whose name has the long-*a* sound in it. Invite other students to do the same.

BUILDING BACKGROUND

Ask students what is happening in the pictures at the top of p. 37. Ask them to talk about what Tom, May, and Pat are doing in each picture. Can they retell what happened in the play on the previous pages without looking back? Invite students to talk about different things they do on a great day in the summer. Review the events of the photo play together.

USING PAGE 37

Read the instructions at the top of p. 37 to the students. Ask what is happening in the pictures. Have students read the sentences quietly to themselves and circle *yes* if the sentence is correct or *no* if it is not. Point out that example 1 has been done for them. Tell students they can turn back and reread the play if they need to check an answer. Recall and memory are not as important in this exercise as referencing and reading for information.

Say It!
Crazy Sentences

Ask students to reread pp. 30–37 and find words with the long-*a* sound, e.g. *stage, age, face, plate, grapes, cake, train, lake, page, waves, snake,* etc. Invite them to make up their own humorous yes/no sentences using these words. (Example: *A grape has a face.*) Have them write ten of these crazy sentences on a piece of paper, exchange papers with other students and read them aloud to a partner.

Write It!
Write Your Own Play

Brainstorm a favorite folktale, myth, or fable with the class and discuss how it might be made into a short play. On the board, list the characters in the tale and write sample dialogue. (Example: the Greek myth of Medusa, the snake-haired gorgon, who turned all who looked at her into stone.) Divide students into groups and have them (1) list other possible stories that they might make into plays; (2) select one from the list; (3) write a short play together. This activity could take several class sessions and could be extended through library research, art projects (props, sets, costumes), field trips to a local theater, and visits to a computer writing lab to make fliers, invitations, and programs.

UNIT 5

Long Vowels: i

Long Vowels: /ī/ i–e

New Words: Mike, ride, bike, like, pie, nine, lines, drive, five, miles

---

Phonics Objectives

Can students:
- ✓ listen for the long-*i* sound?
- ✓ identify the long-*i* sound formed by the letter combination *i–e*?
- ✓ read and write words and sentences with the long-*i* (*i–e*) sound?

Language Acquisition Objectives

Can students:
- ✓ use the verbs *ride, like, drive*?
- ✓ use numbers?

ESL Standards
- • Goal 2, Standard 2

FOCUSING ON PHONEMIC AWARENESS

Say the word *milk*. What is the vowel sound? (short-*i*) Explain that the vowel *i*, like the vowel *a*, can have more than one sound in English. When you add the letter *e* to the end of a short-*i* word, the vowel sound becomes long-*i*. The *e* on the end is silent. Now say *Mike* and model oral blending: *Miiiiike*. Write *Mike* on the board and underline the *i* and silent *e*. Indicate the picture of Mike on p. 38 and repeat the word *Mike*. Stress the long-*i* sound.

USING PAGE 38

Ask students to:
- • point to the letters *i–e*
- • locate words as you say them
- • read aloud and track words with you

Show students how the vowel *i*, a consonant, and the vowel *e* form the long-*i* sound. Point out the long-*i* words in the box at the top of the page that follow the VCV (vowel–consonant–vowel) pattern: *Mike, rides, bike, likes, nine, lines, drive, five*. Explain that the long-*i* sound can also be formed by other letter patterns such as *ie*. Write the word *pie* on the chalkboard.

ACTIVITIES FOR ALL LEARNERS

Long-*i* or Short-*i*?
(Auditory and Visual Learners)

Materials: writing paper, magazine pictures or picture cards of short-*i* and long-*i* words such as a bike, a pie, a mitt, a hill, a hit, a ride, lines, milk, (numbers) nine, six, and five.

Directions: Ask students to fold a piece of notebook paper in half vertically, writing long-*i* words at the top of one column and short-*i* words at the top of the other column. Tell them you will show pictures of both short-*i* and long-*i* words. Ask them to say the word for each picture to themselves. If it has the long-*i* sound, write it in under long-*i* words. If it has the short-*i* sound, write it under short-*i* words.

Read It! 🎧

Play the audiocassette of p. 38. Have students (1) read along and listen to the following lines and (2) repeat them as directed. Check pronunciation of the long-*i* sound carefully.

> Mike rides a bike.
> Mike likes pie.
> nine lines
> Mike drives five miles.
> 1. Mike rides in the rain.
> 2. Mike has five pens.
> 3. Pat likes apple pie.
> 4. Mike drives five miles.
> 5. The time is five past nine.
> 6. The page has nine lines.

Write It!

Write the words *ride, Mike, bike, like, pie, five, nine, lines, miles,* and *drive* on the board. Ask students to make ten new sentences using these words and read their sentences to a partner.

Long Vowels: /ī/ I, -y

New Words: I, my, hi, eyes, smile, fly, sky, cry, cries

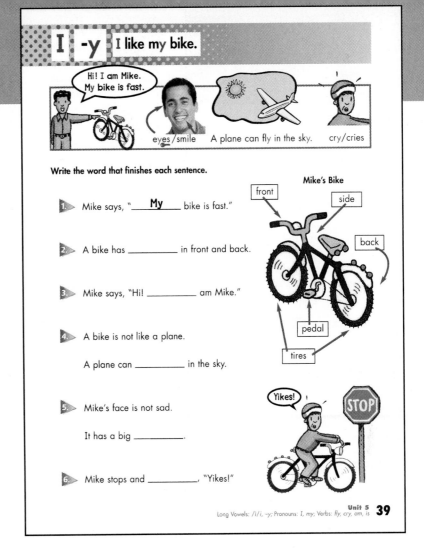

BUILDING BACKGROUND

Write *I* on the chalkboard. Explain that *I* is the subject pronoun used to refer to one-self. Next, say *I am a teacher.* Ask students to tell about themselves by beginning a sentence with *I am . . .* or *I like . . . .*

Write *my* on the chalkboard. Pronounce *my* and have students repeat it after you. Explain that the letter *y* can also stand for the long-*i* sound. Contrast the word *my* (possessive adjective) with the word *me* (object pronoun). New speakers of English sometimes confuse these two words, so you may wish to emphasize the difference.

USING PAGE 39

Ask students to:
- point to the letters *i* and *y*
- locate the long-*i* words as you say them
- read aloud and track words with you

Point to the words *cry/cries* in the box at the top of p. 39. Explain that verbs ending in *y* change to *ies* when conjugated in the

third person singular (*he/she cries*). Write the examples *I cry* and *Mike cries* on the board. Ask students for more examples, such as *I fly; a plane flies; I try; she tries*.

ACTIVITIES FOR ALL LEARNERS

I like . . .; Who am I?
(Visual Learners)

Materials: old catalogs, advertisements from newspapers, scissors, paper, glue

Directions: Ask students to cut out pictures of things they like from catalogs and advertisements. Have them make a poster with the words *I like . . .* surrounded by their favorite items. Instruct them *not* to write their name on the poster. Display the posters on a wall and invite students from another class to look at each poster, notice the items which the student likes, and guess who made that poster.

Read It!

Play the audiocassette of p. 39. Have students (1) read along and

listen to the following lines and (2) repeat them as directed. Check pronunciation of the long-*i* sound carefully.

> Hi! I am Mike. My bike is fast.
> eyes/smile
> A plane can fly in the sky.
> cry/cries
> 1. Mike says, "My bike is fast."
> 2. A bike has tires in front and back.
> 3. Mike says, " Hi! I am Mike."
> 4. A bike is not like a plane.
>   A plane can fly in the sky.
> 5. Mike's face is not sad. It has a big smile.
> 6. Mike stops and cries, "Yikes!"

Write It!
Make a Crossword

Divide the class into pairs and invite students to (1) list the long-*i* words from pp. 38 and 39, and (2) create crossword puzzles using those words. You may wish to use graph paper for this project.

Long Vowels: /ī/ *igh*

New Words: light, night, bright, high, right

Phonics Objectives

Can students:

✓ listen for and identify the long-*i* sound formed by the letter combination *igh*?

✓ read and write words and sentences with the long-*i* sound?

Language Acquisition Objectives

Can students:

✓ use the adjectives *bright, high, right*?

Students:

• use left and right directions

• use the verbs *fly, ride*

ESL Standards

• Goal 2, Standard 1

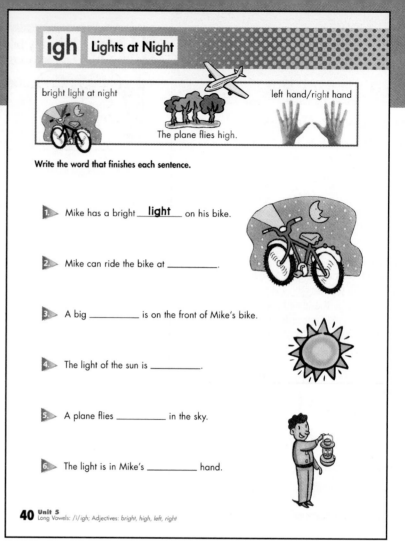

igh Lights at Night

bright light at night | The plane flies high. | left hand/right hand

Write the word that finishes each sentence.

1. Mike has a bright **light** on his bike.

2. Mike can ride the bike at _____.

3. A big _____ is on the front of Mike's bike.

4. The light of the sun is _____.

5. A plane flies _____ in the sky.

6. The light is in Mike's _____ hand.

40 Unit 5
Long Vowels: /i/ *igh*; Adjectives: *bright, high, left, right*

BUILDING BACKGROUND

Write the word *night* on the chalkboard. Underline the *gh* and explain that these letters are silent (not pronounced). Tell students that *i + gh* creates the long-*i* sound. Write the word *light* and pronounce it. Invite students to repeat it after you. Now write *high* and *hi*. Explain that some words in English sound alike but are spelled differently and have different meanings. They are called homonyms.

USING PAGE 40

Ask students to:

• point to the letters

• locate words as you say them

• read aloud and track words with you

Point to the words *bright, high,* and *right* on p. 40. What kind of words are these? (adjectives) Explain that the word *right* has two meanings. *Right* can mean "correct" or *right* can refer to a direction. Illustrate

the directions *right* and *left*. Ask students to explain the words for *right* and *left* in their own languages.

ACTIVITIES FOR ALL LEARNERS

Turn Left, Turn Right!
(Kinesthetic/Auditory Learners)

Materials: scarf to be used as a blindfold

Directions: Demonstrate a blindfold. Ask for two volunteers. Explain that one person will wear a blindfold and the other will be a guide. The guide will give the blindfolded person directions to a place in the classroom (*turn left, turn right, go back, go forward, stop*). Let other students try the game until all have had a chance to practice following directions. The game can be extended to places outside the classroom. When the game is finished, you may wish to discuss blindfold games in other cultures.

Say It!
"Star Light, Star Bright"

Teach the class the following rhyme:

Star light, star bright.
First star I see tonight.
Wish I may. Wish I might.
Have the wish I wish tonight.

Distribute copies of the rhyme on p. 97 and ask students to listen for the long-*i* words and underline them.

Write It!
Quiz Time

Write the following two sentences on the chalkboard.

1. The lights were _____. (*bright, night*)
2. I go to sleep at _____. (*night, light*)

Ask students to copy the sentences on a piece of paper. Have a volunteer fill in the correct word for each sentence. Ask students to make up eight more long-*i* quiz sentences and list them on their paper. When they finish, students can pass the quiz to friends to read and complete.

Long Vowels: /ī/ ire, ice

New Words: fire, ice, tire, wide, sign, mice, hide, bite

Phonics Objectives

Can students:
- ✓ listen for the long-*i* sound (*ire*, *ice*)?
- ✓ identify the long-*i* sound formed by *i* and *-re*, *-ce*?
- ✓ read and write words and sentences with the long-*i* sound (*ire*, *ice*)?

Language Acquisition Objectives

Can students:
- ✓ use the verbs *hide*, *bite*?
- ✓ use the adjectives *wide*, *flat*?

ESL Standards
- Goal 1, Standard 3

ire ice Fire and Ice

fire | ice | a flat tire | a wide sign | Mice hide. | Mice bite.

Circle *yes* if the sentence is true.
Circle *no* if the sentence is not true.

1. A fire is hot.	yes	no
2. Mice can fly in the sky.	yes	no
3. A stop sign is red.	yes	no
4. Ice is hot.	yes	no
5. A dog can bite a ball.	yes	no
6. A sign can bite a light.	yes	no
7. Bikes have nine tires.	yes	no
8. A frog can hide in the grass.	yes	no
9. A pen is wide and big.	yes	no
10. A flat tire can make a bike stop.	yes	no
11. Mice can drive a truck.	yes	no
12. A fire is bright.	yes	no

Long Vowels: /i/ i–e; Verbs: hide, bite **Unit 5 41**

FOCUSING ON PHONEMIC AWARENESS

Pronounce the word *fire*. Model the blending of the letters *ire*. Invite students to repeat the word *fire*. Say *ice* and review the soft-*c* sound. Ask students if they can remember another soft-*c* word. (*face*, *race*) Have them raise their hands if they hear the sounds of *ire* or *ice* in the following words: *tire, wide, hide, bike, mice, bite, light, nice, fire, night, sign,* and *ice*.

USING PAGE 41

Ask students to:
- point to the letters *ire* and *ice*
- locate words as you say them
- read aloud and track words with you

Write the words *bite, hide, ride, drive, fly, cry,* and *like* on the chalkboard. Ask a student to read the words and use gestures to show what they mean. What are these action words called? (verbs)

ACTIVITIES FOR ALL LEARNERS

My Time Line
(Visual Learners)

Materials: white poster paper, colored pencils or markers

Directions: On the board, draw a timeline of the school year with events that occurred during each month. Now explain that students are going to make personal timelines with each year of their lives written on them. Students can consider what major events happened each year, write the events along the timeline and illustrate the events when appropriate.

Read It!

Play the audiocassette of p. 41. Have students (1) read along and listen to the following lines and (2) repeat them as directed. Check pronunciation of the long-*i* sound carefully.

fire, ice, a flat tire, a wide sign
Mice hide. Mice bite.

1. A fire is hot.	yes
2. Mice can fly in the sky.	no
3. A stop sign is red.	yes
4. Ice is hot.	no
5. A dog can bite a ball.	yes
6. A sign can bite a light.	no
7. Bikes have nine tires.	no
8. A frog can hide in the grass.	yes
9. A pen is wide and big.	no
10. A flat tire can make a bike stop.	yes
11. Mice can drive a truck.	no
12. A fire is bright.	yes

Write It!

Ask students to copy the following cloze paragraph and use the words from the top of p. 41 to complete the sentences:

As I ride my bike, I pass a red _____ that says STOP. My bike hits a rock and the _____ gets flat. I have a snack and _____ into an apple. I see a tent and a hot _____. A man tries to _____ in the tent, but I see him. I cannot run. I am as cold as _____. Can I get away?

Long Vowels: /ā/, /ī/, and Short Vowels

New Word: rhymes

Rhymes
Rhymes have the same ending sounds.
Example: *Mike* and *like* rhyme.

~~lake~~	face	man	night
sky	tire	hot	run	train
bag	day	page	wide
sand	snail	class	nine	jog

Read the word. Find a word from the box above that rhymes with it.
Write the rhyming word on the line.

1. take **lake** _____
2. hand _____
3. ride _____
4. race _____
5. van _____
6. flag _____
7. fly _____
8. fire _____
9. line _____

10. dog _____
11. not _____
12. cage _____
13. sun _____
14. rain _____
15. light _____
16. play _____
17. grass _____
18. pail _____

42 Unit 5
Long Vowels: /ā/, /ī/, and Short Vowels; Rhymes

Phonics Objectives

Can students:
- ✓ listen for the long-*a* sound and long-*i* sound?
- ✓ identify the long-*a* sound and long-*i* sound and distinguish them from other vowel sounds?
- ✓ read and write words and sentences with the long-*a* sound and long-*i* sound?

Language Acquisition Objectives

Can students:
- ✓ use and identify rhymes?

ESL Standards

- Goal 2, Standard 2

FOCUSING ON PHONEMIC AWARENESS

Write the names *Jim* and *Tim* on the chalkboard. Ask a volunteer to repeat the names. What sound is the same in these two words? (*im*) Explain that words with the same ending sound are called rhymes. If any two students have names that rhyme, ask them to stand and say their names. Show picture cards or point out classroom objects whose names rhyme.

USING PAGE 42

Ask students to:
- point to the title "Rhymes"
- locate words as you say them
- read aloud and track words with you

Explain that in the exercise on the page students will choose a rhyming word from the word box and write it in the blank. Remind the class that rhymes appear often in poems and songs. You may suggest that students bring in favorite tapes or CD's that have rhyming lines and play them for the class. (Be sure that you listen to the songs before they are played for the class.) After each song ends, ask the students what rhymes they heard in the lyrics.

ACTIVITIES FOR ALL LEARNERS

Find New Rhymes
(Auditory Learners)

Divide the class into pairs or small groups. Let them read aloud the rhyming words which they wrote on p. 42. Then challenge them to find a third word that rhymes with each set. For example, in number 1, for the words *take* and *lake* they could add the word *make* or *snake*. Ask them to list all the additional rhyming words they found. Ask students to share their lists with the class.

Read It! 🎧

Play the audiocassette of p. 42. Have students (1) read along and listen to the following lines and (2) repeat them as directed. Check pronunciation of the long- and short-vowel words.

1. take/lake
2. hand/sand
3. ride/wide
4. race/face
5. van/man
6. flag/bag
7. fly/sky
8. fire/tire
9. line/nine
10. dog/jog
11. not/hot
12. cage/page
13. sun/run
14. rain/train
15. light/night
16. play/day
17. grass/class
18. pail/snail

Write It!

Ask students to make fifteen sentences using two or more rhyming words from p. 42 in each sentence. Explain that they should underline the rhyming words. Write this example on the board: *I take my bike to the lake.* To extend this activity, encourage students to write songs or poetry. They might read their work to the class.

Photo Story: "The Bike Race"

Review Words: bike, Mike, high, bright, I, wide, drive, tire, five, nine, sign, light, ride, night, fly, cry, like, mile, side, yikes, eyes, smile, lines, pie, mice, bite, hide, fire, ice

Phonics Objectives

Can students:
✓ listen for long-*i* sounds?
✓ read long-*i* words in the context of a story?
✓ write words with long-*i*?

Language Acquisition Objectives

Can students:
✓ read words in story context?

ESL Standards

• Goal 1, Standard 2

FOCUSING ON PHONEMIC AWARENESS

Song: "My Bike"

Play the audiocassette of the following song:

A bright red truck
Drives by my bright red bike
My eyes light up
And I smile a mile wide
I fly my bike
In day or night
I ride so fast
That my tires catch fire!

Distribute the lyrics on p. 97. Play the song again, this time inviting the students to sing along. Ask them to listen for all the long-*i* sounds.

USING THE PHOTO STORY

Preview the photo story, "The Bike Race," with your students. Allow the students time to look through the story and examine the pictures and text. Ask students to follow along as you play the audiocassette of the story. Students may wish to track the words as the story is read.

Background discussion: Ask the students if they have a bike. Ask them if they have ever been in a bike race or other competition. Encourage them to relate their own personal experiences. Prompt them with additional questions about sports. What kind of sports do they participate in? Have they ever had an accident during a competition?

Read the photo story together. You may wish to assign volunteers to read (1) the parts of Tom and Mike and Jen; (2) the four narrator parts—one reader for each set of captions under the four pictures. As students read, listen for correct pronuncia-

tion of the long-*i* sounds in the Review Words (above). Do not interrupt the story, but discuss problem words and errors in pronunciation after the reading. Model the correct pronunciations for students and ask them to repeat the words after you.

Review the story. Lead the class in a second reading of "The Bike Race." This time, ask for new volunteers to read aloud. After they finish reading, ask questions focusing on the content of the story:

• Who called Mike? (*Tom*)
• Why can't Tom race today? (*He has a job.*)
• Who can't wait to race? (*Mike and Jen*)
• Who has a black bike? (*Mike*)
• What does the man drop to begin the race? (*a flag*)
• How many bikes race on the hill? (*nine*)
• What does Jen's bike hit? (*a rock*)
• What happens to Jen's front tire? (*It is flat.*)
• Is Jen's leg okay? (*yes*)

Questions

Review Words: bike, Mike, high, bright, I, wide, drive, tire, five, nine, sign, light, ride, night, fly, cry, like, mile, side, yikes, eyes, smile, line, pie, mice, bite, hide, fire, ice

Phonics Objectives

Can students:
- ✓ listen for long-*i* sounds?
- ✓ read long-*i* words in the context of a story?
- ✓ write words with long-*i*?

Language Acquisition Objectives

Students:
- review verbs *ride, fly, like, wait, race, stop*
- use words related to outdoor activities
- recall what they read

ESL Standards
- Goal 2, Standard 1

Questions

~~mile~~	job
rock	fly
nine	help
red	wait
black	tire

Complete the sentences below using a word from the box.

1. The bike race is a five-___**mile**___ race.

2. Mike and Jen can't _____ to race.

3. Mike calls Tom, but Tom has a _____ and can't race.

4. Mike has a _____ bike.

5. Jen has a bright _____ bike.

6. _____ bikes race on the hill.

7. Jen says, "My bike can _____."

8. Jen's bike hits a _____.

9. Jen's bike has a flat _____.

10. Mike stops to _____ Jen.

To discuss:
- Is Mike right to stop and help Jen?
- Can Jen ride on a flat tire?
- Can Tom have a job and race on the same day?

BUILDING BACKGROUND

Ask students what is happening in the picture at the top of p. 44. Ask students to talk about what Mike is doing. Can they retell what happened in the story on the previous page without turning back to look? Invite students to talk about the bike race. Review the events of the photo story together.

USING PAGE 44

Read the instructions on p. 44. Ask a student to describe what is happening in the picture. Explain that the sentences on this page need to be completed with a word from the box at the top. Ask a student to read sentence 1. Ask students to try to complete the rest of the sentences on their own. If they need to check an answer, they can turn back and reread p. 43. Discuss the questions at the bottom of the page.

CONTENT LINKS

SCIENCE

/i/ *i–e*

S.T.A.R. Life Science by S. Bassano and M. Cristison: Addison Wesley Publishing Co., 1992

Achieving Competence in Science by P. Cohen, J. Deutsch, A. Sorrentino: Amsco School Publications, Inc., 1993

/i/ *i–e* /i/ *igh* /i/ *y*

Content Points A by J. Johnston and M. Johnston: Addison Wesley Publishing Co., 1990

    Unit 4: *Measuring Time*
    Unit 5: *Colors of Light*
    Unit 15: *Life Cycles*

Time and Space: A Basic Reader by M. Connelly and J. Sims: Prentice Hall Regents, 1990

Long Vowels: /a/, /i/ and Short Vowels

Phonics Objectives

Can students:
- ✓ listen for the long-*i* sound?
- ✓ identify the long-*i* sound formed by different letter combinations?
- ✓ read and write words with the long-*i* sound?

Students:
- • review short vowels

Language Acquisition Objectives

Can students:
- ✓ use the verbs *like, is, can*?

ESL Standards

- • Goal 1, Standard 1

REVIEW   My Life

Write about yourself.

1. My name is _____.
   name

2. My address is _____.
   address

   _____.

   *Mike Pace
   777 Red Sands Lane
   Dayton, OH 45310*

3. My age is _____.
   age

4. My mom's name is _____.
   Mom's name

5. My dad's name is _____.
   Dad's name

6. I have: __**X**__ a pen   _____ a van   _____ a job
            _____ a car   _____ a truck   _____ a bike
            _____ a dog   _____ a cat   _____ a desk

7. I like to: _____ jog   _____ walk
               _____ play baseball   _____ have a picnic on the sand
               _____ get up at nine o'clock _____ ride a bike
               _____ swim   _____ get up at six o'clock

8. A snack I like is: _____ grapes   _____ milk
                       _____ hot dogs   _____ pie
                       _____ cake   _____ (other)

BUILDING BACKGROUND

Ask students how they usually describe themselves to someone whom they have just met. Do they mention family? Age? Appearance? Likes and dislikes? Interests? Abilities? Invite the class to discuss what personal qualities they think are important. Write their ideas on the board. Explain that in the next activity they will be filling in a page with information about themselves and their life.

USING THE REVIEW PAGE

Ask a volunteer to read sentence 1 aloud to the class (*My name is . . .*). Then ask students to write their full name, address, age, and parents' names on the given lines. Explain that for the remaining sentences on the page they can choose from the answer choices. In the last section about preferred snacks, point out that the word *other* appears at the end, and tell them that this means they can write any

other favorite food in this space. When the pages are complete, students may wish to exchange books with a partner and discuss what they wrote.

ACTIVITIES FOR ALL LEARNERS

Filling out Forms
(Visual Learners)

Bring in copies of a job application form or a driver's license form. Distribute the forms to the class and have students read the items aloud, line by line. Show them how to fill in the required information. You may wish to make a transparency of the form and discuss it using an overhead projector in order to clarify instructions. Explain technical terms or special vocabulary. Ask if any of the students have had experiences filling out forms. Encourage them to describe what they did.

Say It!
I like . . .

Let students work in pairs to create a dialogue or interview about their likes and dislikes. If they need ideas, they might look at the form on p. 45. (Example: *What sports do you like? Why?*) Discuss what other topics they might include (music, clothes, movies, etc.). When students have finished, they can read their dialogues to the class. Ask those listening to identify the words they hear that have the long-*i* sound.

Write It!

Ask students to copy their interview questions (above) and survey other friends and family to find out what foods, music, sports, school subjects, cars, and styles of clothes people around them like. Discuss how they might make a chart of their findings. When the surveys are finished, have students record and display their data. You might wish to take them to a computer lab to graph their results.

Long Vowels: /ō/ o–e, oa

New Words: Joe, boat, float, nose, goat, road, soap, stove

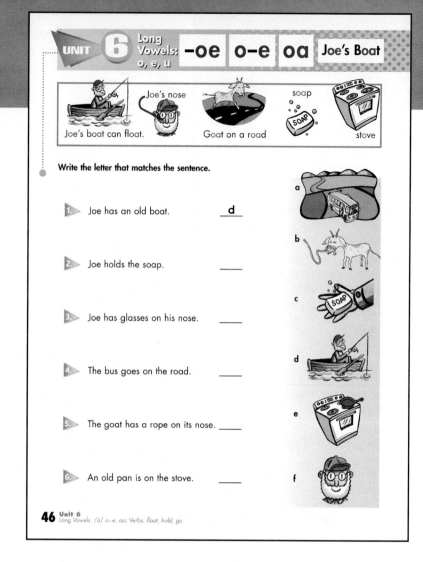

Phonics Objectives

Can students:
✓ listen for the long-*o* sound?
✓ identify the long-*o* sound formed by the letter combinations *o–e* and *oa*?
✓ read and write words and sentences with the long-*o* sound (*o–e*, *oa*)?

Language Acquisition Objectives

Can Students:
✓ use the verbs *hold, go, float*?

ESL Standards
• Goal 2, Standard 1

Focusing on Phonemic Awareness

Say the word *nose*, stressing the long-*o* sound, and point to your nose. Say the word again and model oral blending: *nnnooooossse*. Have the class repeat it after you. Explain that the long-*o* sound can be formed by different letters that combine with *o*, such as *o–e* and *oa*.

Using Page 46

Ask students to:
• point to the letters *o–e* and *oa*
• locate the words as you say them
• read aloud and track words with you

Write *nose* and *soap* on the board. Explain that these words both have the long-*o* sound, but they are spelled differently. Then point out the verb *float* on the page. What other verbs do students see on this page? (*has, holds, goes, is*) Pick up a pen and say, *I can hold the pen.* Pass the pen

to a student and have him/her say the sentence. Then have a volunteer demonstrate the verbs *go* and *float*.

Activities for All Learners

Long-*o* or Short-*o*?
(Kinesthetic/Visual Learners)

Materials: catalogs, magazines, scissors, construction paper, markers

Directions: Divide the class into pairs. Have each pair find long-*o* or and short-*o* objects in the catalogs and magazines. (*coat, rope, mop, log,* etc.) Ask them to sort the objects by sound and make two posters—one with long-*o* words and another with short-*o* words.

Read It!

Play the audiocassette of p. 46. Have students (1) read along and listen to the following lines and (2) repeat them as directed. Check pronunciation of the long-*o* sound carefully.

Joe's boat can float.
Joe's nose
Goat on a road
soap stove
1. Joe has an old boat.
2. Joe holds the soap.
3. Joe has glasses on his nose.
4. The bus goes on the road.
5. The goat has a rope on its nose.
6. An old pan is on the stove.

Write It!

Write *boat, nose, float, rope, stove, goat, road,* and *soap* on the board. Read the following riddles and ask students to write the long-*o* word answers.

• You can climb up me. (*rope*)
• You get clean with me. (*soap*)
• A boat does this. (*float*)
• You smell with me. (*nose*)
• You can row me on a lake. (*boat*)
• You can put a pan on me. (*stove*)
• You can drive a truck on me. (*road*)
• I am an animal with a beard and I like to eat grass. (*goat*)

Long Vowels: /ō/ ow

New Words: slow, yellow, coat, roses, grow, blow, cold, snow, go

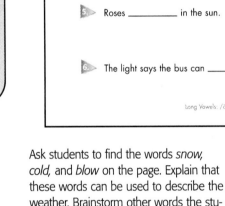

O OW Go Fast/Go Slow

fast boat/slow boat   yellow coat   Roses grow.   Winds blow.   cold snow   stop/go

Write the word that finishes each sentence.

1. A rowboat is a __**slow**__ boat.

2. Joe walks in the _____ and gets cold.

3. Cold winds _____ in the tree.

4. Joe has a _____ coat.

5. Roses _____ in the sun.

6. The light says the bus can _____.

Long Vowels: /ō/o, ow; Verbs: grow, blow, go; Adjectives: fast, slow, cold, yellow   Unit 6 **47**

Focusing on Phonemic Awareness

Say very slowly, *Hello-o-o, stu-u-u-dents*. Ask the students if the words they heard were fast or slow. (*slow*) Say the word *slow* and model oral blending: *sssllllloooow*. Then ask if the word *slow* has the long-*o* sound. Invite students to brainstorm things that are slow. (*snails, slow music, turtles*, etc.)

Ask students to listen as you say some words. If the word has the long-*o* sound as in the word *slow*, they should raise their hands. If not, they should keep their hands down. Use the following words: *plate, blow, grapes, grow, coat, hop, bus, hat, hit, snow, stop, go*.

Using Page 47

Ask students to:
• point to the letters *ow*
• locate the words as you say them
• read aloud and track words with you

Ask students to find the words *snow, cold,* and *blow* on the page. Explain that these words can be used to describe the weather. Brainstorm other words the students know that could be used to indicate weather. (*rain, sun, hot, wind, hail*)

Activities for All Learners

Origami: Folded Paper Boats
(Kinesthetic Learners)

Materials: thin white paper

Directions: Ask if any students know origami. Explain that origami is the Japanese art of folding paper to make objects. Have a student demonstrate how to make a folded paper boat, box, bird, or other object. You may wish to find a book about origami from the library that shows pictures of more complex folded paper objects.

Sing a Long-*o* Song
"Row, Row, Row Your Boat"

 Play the audiocassette of "Row, Row, Row Your Boat." Distribute copies of the lyrics on p. 98 and invite students to underline the words with the long-*o* sound. (*row, boat*) Ask students about their experiences with boats. Have any rowed a boat? Sailed?

Using the Audiocassette

As you play the song again, invite students to sing along. Review the lyrics and be sure students understand the meaning of words like *merrily* and *dream*. Divide the class in two parts and sing the song again as a round. You may wish to choose a student who is a confident singer to lead one part of the round while you lead the other.

Write It!

Ask students to list all the long-*o* words from pp. 46 and 47 on a piece of paper and make sentences using each word. Have them underline the long-*o* word(s) in each sentence they write.

Long Vowels: /ō/ or, oor, oar, our

New Words: more, sports, door, open, floor, scoreboard, corn, four, gold, forks

Phonics Objectives

Can students:
- ✓ listen for the long-o sound?
- ✓ identify the long-o sound formed by the letter combinations or, oor, oar, our?
- ✓ read and write words and sentences with the long-o sound (or, oor, oar, our)?

Language Acquisition Objectives

Can students:
- ✓ use the adjectives more, open, gold?

ESL Standards

- Goal 2, Standard 1

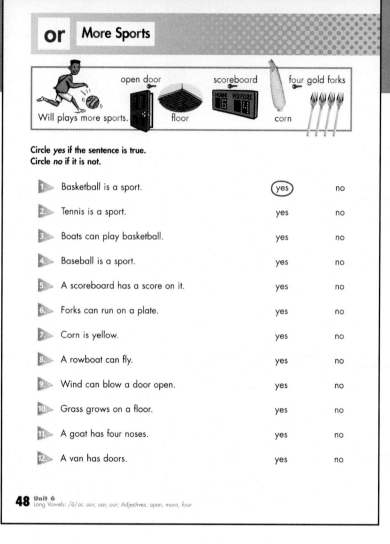

or — More Sports

open door · scoreboard · four gold forks

Will plays more sports. · floor · corn

Circle *yes* if the sentence is true.
Circle *no* if it is not.

		yes	no
1.	Basketball is a sport.	(yes)	no
2.	Tennis is a sport.	yes	no
3.	Boats can play basketball.	yes	no
4.	Baseball is a sport.	yes	no
5.	A scoreboard has a score on it.	yes	no
6.	Forks can run on a plate.	yes	no
7.	Corn is yellow.	yes	no
8.	A rowboat can fly.	yes	no
9.	Wind can blow a door open.	yes	no
10.	Grass grows on a floor.	yes	no
11.	A goat has four noses.	yes	no
12.	A van has doors.	yes	no

48 Unit 6
Long Vowels: /ō/ or, oor, oar, our; Adjectives: open, more, four

BUILDING BACKGROUND

Ask two volunteers to come to the front of the class. Hand student 1 four pens and student 2 six pens. Say, (*student 1's name*) has *four* pens. Ask the class to say it with you. Then say, (*student 2's name*) has *more* pens. Ask the class to say it with you. Ask students to switch pens. Invite volunteers to say the two sentences, reflecting who has four pens and who has more pens. Point out that the words *four* and *more* have the same long-o sound with the letter *r*.

USING PAGE 48

Ask students to:
- point to the letters or, oor, oar, our
- locate the words as you say them
- read aloud and track words with you

Point out the red letters of the words in the box. Read aloud each of the words, emphasizing the /ō/ sound: *more, sports, door, floor, scoreboard, corn, four, forks.*

Ask, *how is the /ō/ sound in these words different from the /ō/ sound in the words open and gold?* Explain that these words all have the long-o sound influenced by the sound of the *r*. Brainstorm with students other words they know that have this sound and make a list on the board.

ACTIVITIES FOR ALL LEARNERS

Sports Report
(Visual/Auditory Learners)

Materials: paper, pens, cardboard microphone

Directions: Divide students into pairs. Explain that they are going to write a one-page sports report and role-play TV reporters, each reading half of the report into the "microphone" in front of the class. The events in the report can be real or fictitious. Encourage students to have fun. They can describe dramatic game plays, their favorite players, bizarre happenings, huge scores, etc.

Say It!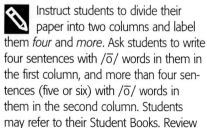

Teach the class the following chant:

Group 1: The baseball score was four to four.
Group 2: The crowd began to roar.
Group 1: Then they scored another four.
Group 2: But we came back with more.

Distribute copies of the chant on p. 98 and ask students to circle words with the /ō/ sound. Divide the class in two groups and repeat the chant again, alternating parts. Discuss the words *crowd* and *roar*.

Write It!

Instruct students to divide their paper into two columns and label them *four* and *more*. Ask students to write four sentences with /ō/ words in them in the first column, and more than four sentences (five or six) with /ō/ words in them in the second column. Students may refer to their Student Books. Review finished work as a class.

Long Vowels: /ō/ and Short Vowels

New Word: low

Phonics Objectives

Can students:
- ✓ listen for the long-*o* sound?
- ✓ identify the long-*o* sound formed by different letter combinations?
- ✓ read and write words and sentences with the long-*o* sound?

Language Acquisition Objectives

Can students:
- ✓ use opposites?

ESL Standards

- Goal 2, Standard 2

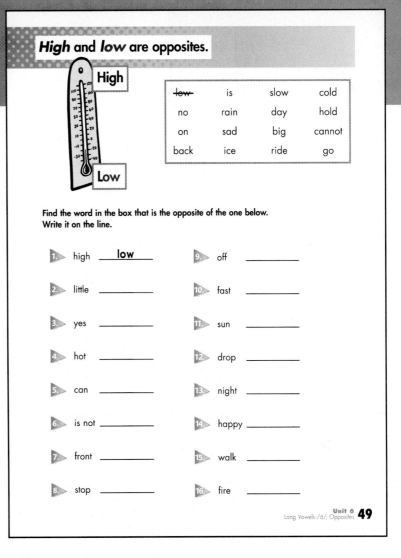

High and **low** are opposites.

~~low~~	is	slow	cold
no	rain	day	hold
on	sad	big	cannot
back	ice	ride	go

Find the word in the box that is the opposite of the one below. Write it on the line.

1. high **low**
2. little _____
3. yes _____
4. hot _____
5. can _____
6. is not _____
7. front _____
8. stop _____

9. off _____
10. fast _____
11. sun _____
12. drop _____
13. night _____
14. happy _____
15. walk _____
16. fire _____

Unit 6
Long Vowels:/ō/; Opposites **49**

BUILDING BACKGROUND

Write *high* at the top of the chalkboard and *low* at the bottom. Ask a volunteer to point out an object that is high and an object that is low in the room. Explain that *high* and *low* refer to opposite locations. Ask students to raise their right hands. What is the opposite hand? (*left*) Say the following words and ask the class to name the opposites: *yes* (*no*), *hot* (*cold*), *near* (*far*), *up* (*down*), *dirty* (*clean*). Can students think of other sets of opposites?

USING PAGE 49

Ask students to:
- point to the letters *ow*
- locate the words as you say them
- read aloud and track words with you

Bring a thermometer to class or borrow one from a science class. Ask students to explain what a thermometer measures. (*temperature*) What is the temperature inside the class? Is it high, low, or medium?

Point to the words *high* and *low* on p. 49. Explain that they refer to the temperature level. Open a newspaper to the weather section and have a student read aloud the high and low temperatures for yesterday. You might ask students to keep a graph of daily temperatures over several weeks, noting the high and low temperatures.

ACTIVITIES FOR ALL LEARNERS

Pictures of Opposites
(Visual Learners)

Materials: old magazines, catalogs, or newspapers, poster paper, scissors, glue

Directions: Divide the class into groups and challenge them to find ten sets of pictures that are opposites, for example, hot/cold, tall/short, big/little, day/night. They may refer to p. 49 for ideas. Have students cut out the sets of pictures, glue them in pairs on the poster paper, and label them. Ask groups to share their posters and explain the sets of opposites. Display the posters.

Say It!
Discussion

Write the following sentence on the chalkboard: *Opposites attract.* Ask students what the saying means. Do they know what a magnet is? Discuss the literal and figurative meaning of the saying. (*Opposite magnetic poles attract; opposite types of people attract.*) Ask students whether they agree or disagree with the saying as it refers to relationships. Do they know any people who are friends although they are very different? Do they have a similar saying about opposites in their own language?

Write It!

Read the following words aloud and ask students to write down the opposite of each word as you say it: *sad* (*happy*), *big* (*little*), *slow* (*fast*), *no* (*yes*), *cold* (*hot*), *can* (*cannot*), *day* (*night*), *front* (*back*), *off* (*on*), *high* (*low*), *go* (*stop*). When you are finished, review the work as a class.

Long Vowels: /ē/ *e–e, ea, ee*

New Words: Steve, read, sleep, tree, leaf, team, eat, meat, green, beans, peas, feet

Phonics Objectives

Can students:
- ✓ listen for the long-*e* sound?
- ✓ identify the long-*e* sound formed by the letter combinations *e–e, ea, ee?*
- ✓ read and write words and sentences with the long-*e* sound (*e–e, ea, ee*)?

Language Acquisition Objectives

Can students:
- ✓ use the verbs *read, sleep, eat?*

ESL Standards

- Goal 2, Standard 1

FOCUSING ON PHONEMIC AWARENESS

Model oral blending of the long-*e* sound in *greeeen* and *seeeee*. Ask students to name things they see that are green. Explain that the long-*e* sound can be formed by different groups of letters such as *e–e, ea, ee*. Tell students to listen as you say the following words and raise their hands if they hear the long-*e* sound: *red, read, mat, meat, sleep, step, tree, see, left, leaf, grape, green, pot, pan, peas, time, team*.

USING PAGE 50

Ask students to:
- point to the letters *e–e, ea,* and *ee*
- locate the words as you say them
- read aloud and track words with you

Point out the words *read, sleep,* and *eat* on p. 50. Ask a student to reread the sentences with these words aloud. Explain that these verbs all have the

long-*e* sound. Engage the students in a discussion of their daily routines. What time do they eat, read, and sleep? Whom do they see each day?

ACTIVITIES FOR ALL LEARNERS

We Read: A Trip to the Library
(Visual/Kinesthetic Learners)

Plan a trip to a library with the class. Discuss favorite books and where to find fiction and non-fiction in a library. If possible, phone the library in advance and schedule the librarian to explain information retrieval systems, locations of collections, etc. Ask a student who has used the library for research purposes to explain what books and articles he/she had to read.

Read It! 🎧

Play the audiocassette of p. 50. Have students (1) read along and listen to the following lines and (2) repeat them as directed. Check pronunciation of the long-*e* sound carefully.

Steve reads.
He sleeps by a tree   leaf
The team eats meat.
green beans and peas   feet
1. Steve reads by a tree.
2. Steve has no socks on his feet.
3. He is on the green team.
4. Steve eats green beans.
5. Bud eats Steve's meat.
6. Steve sleeps till nine o'clock.

Write It!

✏️ Write *read, sleep, tree, leaf, team, eat, meat, green, beans, peas,* and *feet* on the board. Divide the class in pairs and challenge them to write a humorous paragraph containing these words. (*green feet; trees eat meat*) They should (1) brainstorm ideas; (2) make a short outline of the paragraph or list their ideas; (3) write a first draft. Ask students to share their paragraphs. You may wish to edit the paragraphs, return them, and ask students to revise them for display.

Long Vowels: /ē/ *ie*
New Word: field

Phonics Objectives

Can students:
- ✓ listen for the long-*e* sound?
- ✓ identify the long-*e* sound formed by the letter combination *ie*?
- ✓ read and write words and sentences with the long-*e* sound (/ē/, *ie*)?

Language Acquisition Objectives

Can students:
- ✓ use the prepositions *beside, in front of, in back of, behind, above, by, below, between*?

ESL Standards
- Goal 1, Standard 3

---

ie   The Baseball Field

Circle *yes* if the sentence matches the picture.
Circle *no* if it does not.

1.	Jen is beside Mike.	(yes)	no
2.	The flag is above the field.	yes	no
3.	Pat is in front of Steve.	yes	no
4.	The fence is behind the umpire.	yes	no
5.	The umpire is in back of a tree.	yes	no
6.	A boat is above the flag.	yes	no
7.	May is between Tom and Will.	yes	no
8.	Steve is by home plate.	yes	no
9.	A goat is below the tree.	yes	no
10.	Pat is in front of the umpire.	yes	no

Long Vowels: /ē/ie, e-e, ee, e; Prepositions **Unit 6 51**

BUILDING BACKGROUND

Write *behind, in front of, beside* on the board. Stand behind your desk and say, *I am behind my desk.* Step in front of your desk and say, *I am in front of my desk.* Then step to the side of your desk and say, *I am beside my desk.* Invite students to stand up and repeat each sentence with you as they step behind, in front of, and beside their own desks.

USING PAGE 51

Ask students to:
- point to the letters *ie*
- locate the words as you say them
- read aloud and track words with you

Read aloud the title of p. 51, "The Baseball Field," and point out the long-*e* sound in *field*. Explain the prepositions in the scene: *Pat is in front of the umpire. The umpire is in back of/behind Pat. Mike is beside Jen. May is between Will and*

Tom. *The goat is below the tree. The flag is above the field.* Ask students about their favorite baseball teams and players. Encourage discussion to expand oral language.

ACTIVITIES FOR ALL LEARNERS

Listen and Draw
(Visual/Auditory Learners)

Materials: pens or markers, blank paper

Directions: Explain that students are going to sketch objects to illustrate prepositions. They can just use stick figures or simple symbols. Tell them to listen and draw as you read the following directions: *In the middle of the page, draw a large tree. Draw a bird above the tree. Draw a house beside the tree. Draw a small flower between the house and the tree. Draw a snail below the flower. Draw steps by the door of the house. Draw a ball in front of the steps.*

Read It!

Play the audiocassette of p. 51. Have students (1) look at the words at the top of p. 51 and read along silently with the recorded voice; (2) listen carefully as the reader pronounces the long-*e* and long-*o* words; (3) reread the lines, repeating them aloud as instructed. Be sure to check students' pronunciation as they reread.

1. Jen is beside Mike.   yes
2. The flag is above the field.   yes
3. Pat is in front of Steve.   no
4. The fence is behind the umpire.   yes
5. The umpire is in back of a tree.   no
6. A boat is above the flag.   no
7. May is between Tom and Will.   yes
8. Steve is by home plate.   yes
9. A goat is below the tree.   yes
10. Pat is in front of the umpire.   yes

Write It!

Have students write correct sentences in place of the three sentences on p. 51 that do not match the picture.

Long Vowels: /ē/ e, ey, y

New Words: key, funny, monkey, happy, baby, study, sixty, forty, twenty, he, me, easy

Phonics Objectives

Can students:
- ✓ listen for the long-e sound?
- ✓ identify the long-e sound formed by the letter e, the letter y, and the letter combination ey?
- ✓ read and write words and sentences with the long-e sound (e, ey, y)?

Language Acquisition Objectives

Can students:
- ✓ use the pronouns he and me?
- ✓ use the numbers sixty, forty, twenty?

ESL Standards

- Goal 1, Standard 2

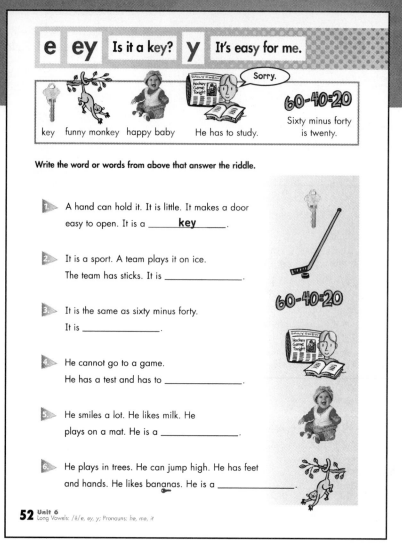

e ey Is it a key? y It's easy for me.

key   funny monkey   happy baby   He has to study.   60-40=20   Sixty minus forty is twenty.

Write the word or words from above that answer the riddle.

1. A hand can hold it. It is little. It makes a door easy to open. It is a _____**key**_____.

2. It is a sport. A team plays it on ice. The team has sticks. It is _____.

3. It is the same as sixty minus forty. It is _____.

4. He cannot go to a game. He has a test and has to _____.

5. He smiles a lot. He likes milk. He plays on a mat. He is a _____.

6. He plays in trees. He can jump high. He has feet and hands. He likes bananas. He is a _____.

52 Unit 6
Long Vowels: /ē/e, ey, y; Pronouns: he, me, it

FOCUSING ON PHONEMIC AWARENESS

Tell students to listen carefully as you say the following words: *happy, baby, monkey*. What sound do these words have in common? Explain that sometimes y or ey stands for the long-e sound at the end of a word. Say the following list of words and ask students to raise their hands if the word has the long-e sound: *monkey, man, baby, pretty, little, money, funny, six, sixty, four, forty, twenty*.

USING PAGE 52

Ask students to:
- point to the letters e, ey, and y
- locate the words as you say them
- read aloud and track words with you

Point to the pronouns *he* and *me* on p. 52. Write, *Steve reads* on the board. Erase *Steve* and write *He* in its place. Explain that *he* is a subject pronoun and can take the place of a male name in a sentence. Next, write *me* on the board.

Hand a student a book and say, *Please give the book to me.* Explain that *me* is an object pronoun. Have students take turns creating sentences that use the pronouns *he* and *me*.

ACTIVITIES FOR ALL LEARNERS

Study Skills
(Visual/Auditory Learners)

Ask students how they study a chapter to prepare for a test. List the strategies on the board. You may wish to include the following study skills: (1) underline key words and definitions; (2) list main ideas; (3) take notes; (4) summarize; (5) discuss the chapter with a friend; (6) create questions to test yourself.

Song: "Rock-a-Bye Baby"

Play the audiocassette of "Rock-a-Bye Baby." Distribute copies of the lyrics on p. 98 and invite students to underline the words with long-e, -a, and -o sounds. (*baby, tree, blows, cradle, breaks*) Explain that this song is a lullaby. Ask stu-

dents if they know lullabies in other languages.

USING THE AUDIOCASSETTE

As you play the song again, invite students to sing along. Review the lyrics and be sure students understand the meaning of words like *bough* and *cradle*.

Write It!
Riddles

Divide the class into pairs. Ask students to reread the riddles on p. 52. Point out that they are written as a series of sentences with a blank at the end. Have students brainstorm ten riddles of their own and write them on a piece of paper. (Example: *It is a sport. It has a high net and a ball. Five people play it. It is _____.*) They may wish to look back on previous pages for ideas. When they finish, they can ask their riddles to another pair of students.

Long Vowels: /ē/ eer, ear

New Words: deer, near, ear, hear, see, tears, years, beard

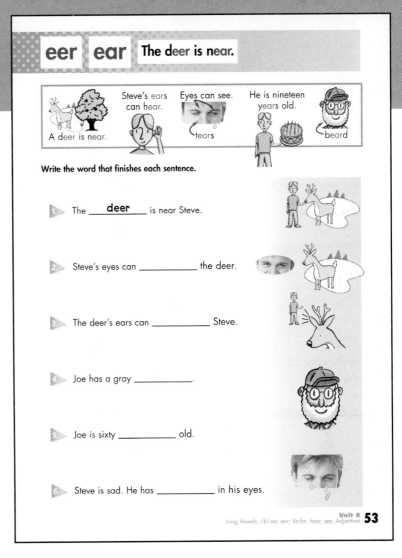

eer | ear   The deer is near.

Steve's ears can hear.
Eyes can see. tears
He is nineteen years old. beard
A deer is near.

Write the word that finishes each sentence.

1. The _____deer_____ is near Steve.

2. Steve's eyes can _____ the deer.

3. The deer's ears can _____ Steve.

4. Joe has a gray _____.

5. Joe is sixty _____ old.

6. Steve is sad. He has _____ in his eyes.

Long Vowels: /ē/ eer, ear; Verbs: hear, see; Adjectives **53**

FOCUSING ON PHONEMIC AWARENESS

Ask a student to tell you his/her age. Then say, (student's name) *is (age) years old.* Ask if *year* has the long-e sound. Go around the class and let everyone say how old he or she is with the sentence, *I am _____ years old.* Say the word *ears* slowly, blending the sounds *eeeear* and indicating your ear. Ask students to listen as you say the following words and raise their hands if they hear the long-e sound: *deer, door, fire, fear, tire, tear, beard, year, near, floor, more, hear.*

USING PAGE 53

Ask students to:
• point to the letters *eer* and *ear*
• locate the words as you say them
• read aloud and track words with you

Point out the verbs *hear* and *see*. Explain that these verbs describe senses. Ask students what other sensory verbs they know.

(*smell, feel*) Indicate the adjectives *near* and *nineteen*. Ask students to name other adjectives they know. (*big, red, four, flat*)

ACTIVITIES FOR ALL LEARNERS

Game: Near/Not Near
(Kinesthetic/Auditory Learners)

Tell students that you are thinking of something in the classroom. The object of the game is to try to figure out what it is that you have chosen. Ask a volunteer to walk around the room. Say *near* if the student approaches the item. Say *not near* when the student moves away from it. The student will continue to move *near* and *not near* until he/she names the object. After the student guesses the object correctly, he/she chooses the next item and the game continues.

Song: "Home on the Range"

Play the audiocassette of "Home on the Range." Distribute copies of the lyrics on p. 98 and invite students to

underline the words with the long-e and long-o sounds. (*me, deer, oh, home, buffalo, roam, antelope*) What other long vowels do students hear? (long-*a*: *play, day, range;* long-*i*: *skies*)

USING THE AUDIOCASSETTE

As you play the song again, invite students to sing along. Review the lyrics and be sure students understand words like *roam, antelope, heard, discouraging, cloudy,* and *range.*

Write It!
Long-e or Short-e

Review the long-e words on pp. 50–53 (*deer, near, ear, hear,* etc.) and the short-e words on pp. 14–15 (*leg, bed, red, wet,* etc.). Ask students to write eight sentences using both long-e words and short-e words, for example: *The deer runs in the rain and gets wet.* Have students underline long-e words twice and short-e words once.

Long Vowels: /ü/ *ue, u–e*

New Words: Luz, tune, flute, use, glue, blue, June, huge, cube, music

Phonics Objectives

Can students:
- ✓ listen for the long-*u* sound?
- ✓ identify the long-*u* sound formed by the letter combinations *ue, u–e*?
- ✓ read and write words and sentences with the long-*u* sound (*ue, u–e*)?

Language Acquisition Objectives

Can students:
- ✓ use words relating to music: *tune, flute*?
- ✓ use the verb *use*?

ESL Standards

- Goal 2, Standard 1

FOCUSING ON PHONEMIC AWARENESS

Model blending of the sounds of *bl* and *ue*: *bluuuue*. Tell the class that the /ü/ sound in *blue* is called the long-*u* sound. Explain that the long-*u* sound can be formed by the letters *u, ue,* or *u–e*. Mention that the /u/ sound in *huge* is a variation of the long-*u* sound. Say the word *huge* and model oral blending: *huuuuge*. Ask students to listen carefully as you say the following words and raise their hands if they hear the long-*u* sound as in *blue* or *cube*: <u>flute</u>, <u>huge</u>, bug, bag, sand, bus, <u>Luz</u>, get, <u>glue</u>, <u>tune</u>, take, sky, jog, <u>June</u>.

USING PAGE 54

Ask students to:
- point to the letters *ue, u–e*
- locate the words as you say them
- read aloud and track words with you

Hum a familiar tune for the class, such as "This Land Is Your Land" or "Swing Low, Sweet Chariot." Ask if anyone can identify the tune. Point out the sentence *Luz plays a tune on the flute* on p. 54. Ask what a tune is. (*song or melody*) Ask if anyone in the class plays a small instrument. Invite him/her to bring it to class.

Indicate the red letters in the words in the box on p. 54 and explain how *u, ue,* and *u–e* all stand for the long-*u* sound.

ACTIVITIES FOR ALL LEARNERS

Favorite Music
(Auditory Learners)

Materials: audiocassette or CD player

Directions: Ask students what their favorite kind of music is. (*rock, rap, reggae, classical, salsa, country*) Suggest that each student bring in some music to play for the group. If the lyrics are in English, suggest that the student try to transcribe them and make copies for the class.

Read It! 🎧

Play the audiocassette of p. 54. Have students (1) read along and listen to the following lines and (2) repeat them as directed. Check pronunciation of the long-*u* sound carefully.

> Luz plays a tune on the flute. music
> Luz uses the glue.
> The sky is blue in June.
> a huge cube
> 1. Luz has a blue flute.
> 2. A rainy sky is not blue.
> 3. Luz reads lines of music.
> 4. Luz uses the glue.
> 5. The glass has ice cubes in it.
> 6. Luz likes roses in June.

Write It!

Dictate the following long-*u* words for the students to write: *flute, blue, tune, use, glue, huge, cube, June*. Ask students to write a sentence using each long-*u* word. Review the sentences together.

Long Vowels: /ü/ *ou, ui*

New Words: do, you, soup, juice, two, group, fruit

---

ou Do you...?

Do you like soup? Yes, I do. No, I do not (don't).

juice Two groups of fruit

Circle *yes* if you do. Circle *no* if you do not.

1. Do you like fruit? — (Yes, I do.) — No, I don't.
2. Do you like grape juice? — Yes, I do. — No, I don't.
3. Do you like to play baseball? — Yes, I do. — No, I don't.
4. Do you walk to class? — Yes, I do. — No, I don't.
5. Do you have a job? — Yes, I do. — No, I don't.
6. Do you drive? — Yes, I do. — No, I don't.
7. Do you ride the bus? — Yes, I do. — No, I don't.
8. Do you help at home? — Yes, I do. — No, I don't.
9. Do you play basketball? — Yes, I do. — No, I don't.
10. Do you sit in the front of the class? — Yes, I do. — No, I don't.
11. Do you play music? — Yes, I do. — No, I don't.
12. Do you get up at 7:00? — Yes, I do. — No, I don't.

Long Vowels: /ü/ ou, ui, u; Pronoun: you; Questions with Do you...?; Contraction: don't **55**

BUILDING BACKGROUND

Write *Do you . . .* on the board and say it aloud. Ask students to repeat it. Explain that *Do you* begins a question and is followed by a verb, for example, *Do you like sports? Do you have a pen? Do you want to take the bus?* Explain that you can answer *Yes, I do* or *No, I do not.* Point out that another way to say *do not* is to use the contraction *don't.* After the student has answered, have him/her ask another student a question beginning with *Do you . . . ?* Continue until all the students have asked and answered a question beginning with *Do you . . . .*

USING PAGE 55

Ask students to:

• point to the letters *ou, ui*
• locate the words as you say them
• read aloud and track words with you

Point out to students how the letters *ou* and *ui* form the /ü/ sound in words such

as *you* on the page. Explain that *you* can be either a subject or an object pronoun. Tell the class that when they are talking directly to someone, they use *you* instead of the person's name. Then demonstrate pronouns by pointing at yourself (*I/me*), at another (*you/you*), at a boy (*he/him*); at a girl (*she/her*), at yourself and another (*we/us*), and at others (*they/them*).

ACTIVITIES FOR ALL LEARNERS

Questionnaires: *Do you . . . ?*
(Visual/Kinesthetic Learners)

Brainstorm with the class different *Do you . . .* questions that you might use in an interview. *(Do you like . . . ? When do you . . . ? What do you . . . ?)* Write down their suggestions. Create a questionnaire or interview chart. Have students provide answer lines for responses *yes* or *no.* Ask students to complete the questionnaires by interviewing their friends. Review the results as a class.

Say It! 🎧

Teach the class the following chant:

Group 1: Do you like soup?
Group 2: Yes, I do. I really like soup. Do you?
Group 1: No, I don't. I really don't. But I like juice. Do you?
Group 2: Yes, I like juice
And I like soup.
I really like soup.
Why don't you?

Distribute copies of the chant on p. 98 and ask students to circle words with the /ü/ sound. Divide the class in two groups and repeat the chant again, alternating parts.

Write It!
Dictation from Page 55

Tell the students to study p. 55 for homework. Explain that you will choose 10 of the 12 questions for a dictation. On the following day, ask students to write the 10 questions and their answers as you dictate to them.

Long Vowels: /ū/ ew
New Words: new, few

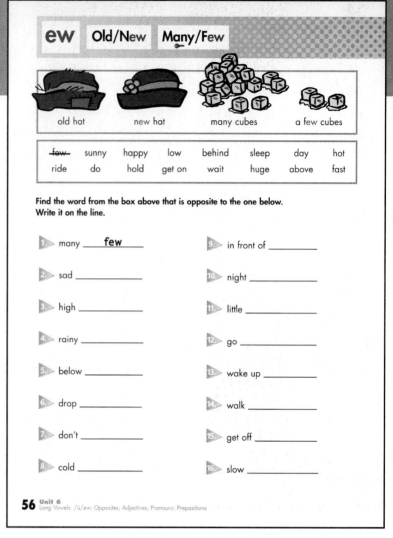

ew	Old/New	Many/Few

old hat   new hat   many cubes   a few cubes

~~few~~	sunny	happy	low	behind	sleep	day	hot
ride	do	hold	get on	wait	huge	above	fast

Find the word from the box above that is opposite to the one below. Write it on the line.

1. many   **few** _____

2. sad _____

3. high _____

4. rainy _____

5. below _____

6. drop _____

7. don't _____

8. cold _____

9. in front of _____

10. night _____

11. little _____

12. go _____

13. wake up _____

14. walk _____

15. get off _____

16. slow _____

56 Unit 6
Long Vowels: /ū/ew; Opposites; Adjectives; Pronouns; Prepositions

---

FOCUSING ON PHONEMIC AWARENESS

Pronounce the words *new, few, cubes* slowly, stressing the /ū/ sound. Ask students to repeat the words. Then say the words *Luz, flute, soup*, stressing the /ü/ sound, and ask students to repeat the words. How are the long-*u* sounds different in these two sets of words (/ū/ and /ü/)? Explain that the /ū/ sound begins with the sound of *y* and sounds like the pronoun *you*. The /ü/ sound is the same as *ou* in *soup*.

USING PAGE 56

Ask students to:
• point to the letters *ew*
• locate the words as you say them
• read aloud and track words with you

Point out the opposite pairs in the title of the page (*old/new, many/few*). Hold up a new book and an old book and explain the meanings. Emphasize that *new* and

old are opposites. Then display a large pile of books (*many books*) beside three books (*a few books*). Tell students that they are adjectives that denote number. *Many* and *few* can also stand alone as pronouns. Review other sets of opposites that students have learned, for example, *high/low, happy/sad,* and *hot/cold.*

ACTIVITIES FOR ALL LEARNERS

A Collage of Opposites
(Visual Learners)

Materials: magazines, catalogs, or newspapers, scissors, glue, blank paper

Directions: Divide the class into pairs or small groups and distribute the materials. Ask students to (1) fold two papers in half vertically; (2) label the two halves of one paper *old* and *new*; (3) label the two halves of the other paper *many* and *few*. Have students cut out pictures from the magazines, catalogs, or newspapers for each category and glue them in place—items that are old/new on one paper and

sets of many/few on the other. Have students share and explain their collages.

Say It!
An Old Rhyme

Teach the following traditional rhyme from England:

> Something old
> Something new
> Something borrowed
> Something blue
> Silver sixpence* in your shoe.

Explain that this rhyme tells what a bride is supposed to wear for good luck on her wedding day. Ask students about wedding customs in other countries. Distribute copies of p. 98 and ask students to circle the long-*u* words.

Write It!
Sentences

Ask students to write a sentence using each word that they wrote as an opposite on p. 56. Have them underline the given word in each sentence. (Example 2, sad/happy: *He is* <u>*happy*</u> *today.*)

* Old English coin

Photo Play: "Home Run"

Review Words: Steve, green, team, he, see, hear, Luz, easy, leaves, behind, tree, low, slow, float, near, go, home, field, scoreboard, four

Phonics Objectives

Can students:
- ✓ listen for the long-*o*, -*e*, and -*u* sounds?
- ✓ read words with the long vowels *o*, *e*, and *u* in the context of a story?
- ✓ write words with the long vowels *o*, *e*, *u*?

Language Acquisition Objectives

Can students:
- ✓ read words in story context?

ESL Standards
- Goal 3, Standard 2

Home Run

Names in the play: Luz, Pat, Mike, Jen, Steve, Tom, Will, May, Umpire, Narrator

Narrator: The green team is at bat. Luz, Pat, and Mike have hits and wait on the bases. Steve steps up to the plate.

Jen:	Go, Steve!
May:	You can do it, Steve!
Steve:	Okay. [*to Jen*] Can you see the big tree?
Jen:	You mean the tree behind the fence?
Steve:	Right.
Jen:	Yes, I see it. Can you hit it?
Steve:	Easy. Wait and see.
Jen:	Do it, Steve! Hit the tree!
May:	Go for it, Steve!

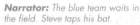

Narrator: The blue team waits in the field. Steve taps his bat.

Umpire:	Ball one.
Tom:	Wide and low.
Will:	Let the low ones go, Steve.
Narrator:	*A slow ball floats in low.*
Umpire:	Ball two!
Will:	Wait for the right one, Steve!
Jen:	Yes, wait for a high one.
Steve:	Come on. Let's have it. Time for a fast ball.
Umpire:	Strike one!

Unit 6
Long Vowels: *o, e, u* **57**

FOCUSING ON PHONEMIC AWARENESS

Sing a Song
"Take Me Out to the Ball Game" 🎧

🎵 Play the audiocassette of "Take Me Out to the Ball Game." Distribute copies of the lyrics on p. 98 and invite students to underline the words with the long-*e*, -*o*, and -*u* sounds. (*me, peanuts, team, three, don't, home, old*) What other long vowels do they hear? (long-*a: take, game, shame*; long-*i: I, buy, strikes*)

USING THE AUDIOCASSETTE 🎧

As you play the song again, invite students to sing along. Review the lyrics and be sure students understand statements like *You're out* and *Root for the home team.*

USING THE PHOTO PLAY

🎧 **Preview** the photo play, "Home Run," with your students. Allow students time to look through the play and examine the pictures and text. Ask students to follow along as you play the audiocassette. Students may wish to track the words as the play is read.

Background discussion: Ask the students if they have ever played baseball. Have they ever watched a baseball game? Encourage them to relate their own personal experiences. Prompt them with additional questions about sports in their own country. Have they ever scored an important point?

Read the photo play together. Assign volunteers to read the parts of Jen, May, Steve, the umpire, Tom, Will, Mike, Pat, and the narrator. As students read their parts, listen for correct pronunciation of the long-*e*, long-*o*, and long-*u* sounds in the Review Words (above). Do not interrupt the dialogue, but discuss problem words and errors in pronunciation after the

reading. Model the correct pronunciations for students and ask them to repeat the words after you.

Review the play. Lead the class in a second reading of "Home Run." This time, ask new volunteers to read the parts or have the same readers switch parts. After they finish reading, ask questions focusing on the content of the story:

- Which team is at bat? (*the green team*)
- Who is on base? (*Luz, Pat, and Mike*)
- Who steps up to the plate? (*Steve*)
- What is behind the fence? (*a big tree*)
- What team is in the field? (*the blue team*)
- How many strikes does Steve have? (*two*)
- How many balls does he have? (*two*)
- Does the next ball come in fast or slow? (*fast*)
- Where does the ball go when Steve hits it? (*past the fence, in the tree*)
- What is the score at the end? (*six-to-five*)
- What team wins? (*the green team*)

ACTIVITIES FOR ALL LEARNERS

Act Out the Play: "Home Run"
(Kinesthetic/Auditory Learners)

Materials: three paper bases and a home plate, a plastic baseball bat, a sponge-rubber baseball, face masks and chest guards for the catcher and umpire, a paper scoreboard with the score *Home: 6, Visitors: 5*

Directions: Assign the roles of Jen, May, Steve, the umpire, Tom, Will, Mike, Pat, the narrator, a prop person, a catcher, pitcher, and three basemen for the blue team.

Go to a large room like an auditorium or gym with enough space to play baseball. Set up the bases and home plate—center— and three chairs for the green team to the left. Position the blue team catcher, pitcher, and three basemen in the "field." May, Jen, and Will sit in the dugout chairs. Luz is on first base, Pat is on second, and Mike is on third. Steve picks up the bat as the narrator begins. During the dialogue, the pitcher throws balls and strikes as indicated in the script and the umpire makes calls. Practice the play several times, then perform it for others.

Baseball Relay Game
(Kinesthetic/Visual Learners)

Materials: picture cards or pictures of long-*o*, -*e*, and -*u* words; four chairs

Directions: Set up four chairs around the room: three chairs at bases 1, 2, and 3 and the fourth chair at home plate. Divide the class into baseball teams. Then show the pictures. The first team to call out the correct word advances one base. One player from each team moves from home plate to first, then second, then third base, and then back to home. Each time a team reaches home plate, it scores a point.

Narrator: *Steve leaves the box. He taps the bat and faces the plate.*

Umpire: Play ball!

Will: You can do it, Steve.

Jen: Hit it away, Steve.

Umpire: Strike two!

May: Oh, no! Two strikes.

Will: And two balls. Four balls and he walks in a run.

Mike: Hit me in, Steve!

Narrator: *The ball comes in fast. Steve steps up. He hits a high fly.*

Will: Come on home, Mike! Run, Pat! Run, Luz!

Narrator: *The ball floats high above the field. It goes past the fence and lands ... in the tree.*

May: It's in the tree. Run, Steve! You hit the tree!

Umpire: SAFE!

Jen: It's a home run! Come on in, Pat!

Umpire: SAFE!

Narrator: *Luz runs past two bases, down the line and jumps on home plate. Steve jogs in. His hands go up high and a smile is on his face.*

Pat: See the scoreboard? Six-to-five.

All the team: We win! Let's hear it for the green team!

58 Unit 6
Long Vowels: o, e, u

Write It!

Challenge the students to look through the text of the play "Home Run" and underline all the words that have the long-*o*, long-*e*, or long-*u* sounds. Ask students to write lists of these underlined words by sound. When they are finished, review the lists as a class.

CONTENT LINKS

MUSIC

/u/ *u–e, ue,* /o/ *o, o–e,* or /e/ *ee*

Music: Its Role and Importance in Our Lives by Charles Fowler: Glencoe/McGraw-Hill, 1994

Virtuoso Performers: Louis Armstrong
Religious Music: Hinduism, Buddhism, Judaism
Three Musical Creators: Aaron Copland, Duke Ellington, Libby Larsen
Moving Within the Circle: Contemporary Native American Music and Dance by Bryan Burton: World Music Press, 1993

/u/ *u*

Musical Instruments of the World: An Illustrated Encyclopedia by the Diagram Group: Sterling Publishing Co., 1997

Long Vowels: o, e, u

Questions

green	low	slow
tree	wide	ball
plate	strikes	field
floats	go	by
home	wait	blue

Use ten words from the box to finish the sentences.

1. The _____**green**_____ team is at bat.

2. The blue team is in the _____.

3. Steve steps up to the _____ and taps his bat.

4. May says, "_____ for it, Steve!"

5. Ball one is _____ and low.

6. Will yells, "_____ for the right one, Steve!"

7. Steve gets two balls and two _____.

8. Steve hits the fast ball and it _____ high above the field.

9. The ball lands in the big _____ behind the fence.

10. Jen cries, "It's a _____ run!"

Building Background

Ask students what is happening in the picture at the top of p. 59. Invite them to talk about what each character is doing. Can they retell the events of the play? Invite students to talk about baseball games they have played. Have they ever hit a home run? Review the photo play together.

Using Page 59

Read the instructions on p. 59 to the students. Invite a volunteer to read the words in the box under the picture. Explain that these are words from the play. Ask a student to read the example sentence, *The green team is at bat.* Suggest that, as students read each sentence, they try to remember the story and complete the sentence with an appropriate word from the box. If they need to check an answer, they can turn back and reread.

Read It!

Play the audiocassette of p. 59. Have students (1) look at the words at the top of p. 59 and read along silently with the recorded voice; (2) listen carefully as the reader pronounces the long-*o*, -*e*, and -*u* words; (3) reread the lines, repeating them aloud as instructed. Be sure to check students' pronunciation as they reread.

1. The green team is at bat.
2. The blue team is in the field.
3. Steve steps up to the plate and taps his bat.
4. May says, "Go for it, Steve!"
5. Ball one is wide and low.
6. Will yells, "Wait for the right one, Steve!"
7. Steve gets two balls and two strikes.
8. Steve hits the fast ball and it floats high above the field.
9. The ball lands in the big tree behind the fence.
10. Jen cries, "It's a home run!"

Write It!
Partner Dictation

After partners correct their answers to p. 59 (see above), ask one partner to be the "teacher" and dictate the completed sentences to the other partner. As you walk around during this activity, listen for correct pronunciations of the long vowels. Note: This activity also serves as an assessment. You may note which long vowel sounds are causing difficulty for students through their misspellings.

UNIT 7

Digraphs: sh, ph, th

Digraphs: /sh/ *sh*

New Words: she, shop, shoes, wash, dish, brush, shelf, fish, shave

---

Phonics Objectives

Can students:
- ✓ listen for and identify the /sh/ sound formed by the letter combination *sh*?
- ✓ read and write words and sentences with the /sh/ sound?

Language Acquisition Objectives

Can students:
- ✓ use the verbs *shop, wash, shave*?

ESL Standards

• Goal 2, Standard 1

She shops for shoes.   She washes dishes.   brush on a shelf   fish   He shaves.   shoes

Write the letter that matches the sentence.

1. She shops for new black shoes.   d
2. Four sheep eat grass.   ____
3. He wakes up at 6:00 and shaves.   ____
4. Wash your hands before you eat.   ____
5. The dish has a fish on it.   ____
6. A belt is on the shelf.   ____

a b c d e f

60 Unit 7
Digraphs: /sh/sh; Verbs: wash, shop, shave

FOCUSING ON PHONEMIC AWARENESS

Say *shhhhhhh*. Ask students what this sound often means in English. (*be quiet*) Have them listen carefully as you say *sh* again. Point out that the /sh/ sound may be at the beginning, middle, or end of a word, as in *shop, washes,* or *brush*. Ask students to listen to the following words and raise their hands if they hear the /sh/ sound: *shoes, see, shop, wet, wash, fit, fish, bus, brush, stay, say, shave, sell, shell, shelf.*

USING PAGE 60

Ask students to:
• point to the letters *sh*
• locate the words as you say them
• read aloud and track words with you

Read the title: *She likes to shop.* Point out how the *sh* letters stand for the /sh/ sound. Ask students to read the sentences and words at the top of p. 60 as you read

them aloud. Have students repeat the words after you. Ask a volunteer to explain the words *shop, wash,* and *shave.*

ACTIVITIES FOR ALL LEARNERS

Shopping Lists
(Visual Learners)

Materials: grocery advertisement sections from newspapers, paper, pencils

Directions: Divide students into pairs. Explain that they are going to make shopping lists based on food items that are on sale in the newspaper. Distribute the grocery advertisement sections. Ask students to find twenty items they like or need and write them on their shopping list. When they finish, have students compare shopping lists.

Read It!

Play the audiocassette of p. 60. Have students (1) read along and listen to the following lines and (2) repeat them as directed. Check pronunciation of

the /sh/ words carefully.

> She shops for shoes. shoes
> She washes dishes.
> brush on a shelf
> fish He shaves.
> 1. She shops for new black shoes.
> 2. Four sheep eat grass.
> 3. He wakes up at 6:00 and shaves.
> 4. Wash your hands before you eat.
> 5. The dish has a fish on it.
> 6. A belt is on the shelf.

Write It!

Read these riddles to the class. After each riddle, ask students to write down the *sh* word answer from p. 60.

• You do this to clean your face. (*wash*)
• You use this to make your hair neat. (*brush*)
• You wear these on your feet. (*shoes*)
• Cats like to eat this. (*fish*)
• This animal eats grass. (*sheep*)
• This is like a plate. (*dish*)
• You can put books on this. (*shelf*)
• You do this in a store. (*shop*)

Digraphs: /f/ *ph*

New Words: telephone/phone, earphones, graph, phonics, photo, elephant

ph On the Phone

telephone   earphones   graph   Phonics Team photo   elephant

Fill in the phone conversation. Write the words that finish each sentence.

Steve: Hi, Mike.

Mike: Hi, Steve.

Steve: Do you want to play ___baseball___?
baseball/brush

Mike: Sure. Do you have your new _____?
graph/bat

Steve: Yes. Do you have your _____?
mitt/fish

Mike: Yes. Let's phone May to see if _____ can play.
she/he

Steve: She has to baby-sit. She _____ play.
can/can't

Mike: Okay. Let's play on the _____ next to your road.
field/photo

Steve: Fine. Can you ride your _____ here?
earphones/bike

Mike: Sure. See you in ten minutes.

Steve: Okay. Bye, Mike.

Mike: Bye.

Digraphs: /f/ph; Questions with *Do you...?* **Unit 7 61**

BUILDING BACKGROUND

Ask students to repeat the words *phone* and *telephone* with you, stressing the /f/ sound. Ask how often they talk on the telephone. To whom do they talk?

Invite two volunteers to come to the front of the class and have a mock phone conversation using imaginary phones. Suggest they talk about weekend plans. Challenge them to improvise. When they are finished, brainstorm other topics for phone conversations and invite other volunteers to practice talking on the phone.

USING PAGE 61

Ask students to:
- point to the letters *ph*
- locate the words as you say them
- read aloud and track words with you

Point to the word *phone* in the title on p. 60 and explain that, in English, the letters *ph* often stand for the same sound

as the letter *f*. Say the /f/ sound. Tell students that the /f/ sound can be at the beginning, middle, or end of words and ask students to point out examples on the page. (*phone, elephant, graph*)

ACTIVITIES FOR ALL LEARNERS

Write Phone Dialogues
(Auditory Learners)

Tell students to think of things they might talk about on the phone. Write a list of their ideas on the board. Then invite them to write their own phone dialogues about a topic they choose. Volunteers can read their dialogues with their partners to the class.

Read It! 🎧

Play the audiocassette of p. 61. Have students (1) read along and listen to the following lines and (2) repeat them as directed. Check pronunciation of the *ph* words carefully.

telephone earphones graph
Phonics Team photo elephant

Hi, Mike.
Hi, Steve.
Do you want to play baseball?
Sure. Do you have your new bat?
Yes. Do you have your mitt?
Yes. Let's phone May to see if
  she can play.
She has to baby-sit. She can't play.
Okay. Let's play on the field next
  to your road.
Fine. Can you ride your bike here?
Sure. See you in ten minutes.
Okay. Bye, Mike.
Bye.

Write It!

Ask students to make a crossword puzzle that includes some of the following words: *elephant, graph, telephone, earphones, phonics, photo,* and other New Words. You may wish to distribute graph paper and show a sample puzzle done on the graph paper. Photocopy sets of finished puzzles for students to do.

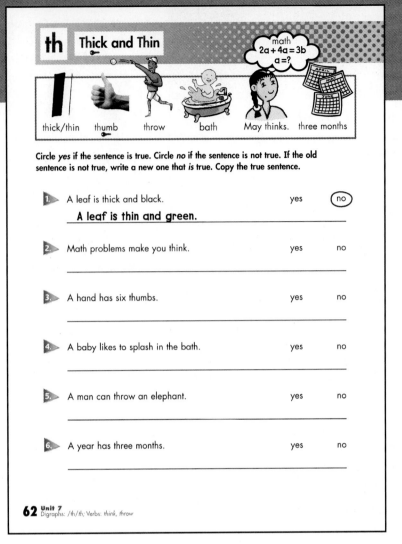

Digraphs: /th/ *th* (voiceless)

New Words: thick, thin, thumb, throw, bath, think, math, three, month

th Thick and Thin

Circle *yes* if the sentence is true. Circle *no* if the sentence is not true. If the old sentence is not true, write a new one that *is* true. Copy the true sentence.

1. A leaf is thick and black. yes (no)
   A leaf is thin and green.
2. Math problems make you think. yes no
3. A hand has six thumbs. yes no
4. A baby likes to splash in the bath. yes no
5. A man can throw an elephant. yes no
6. A year has three months. yes no

62 Unit 7 Digraphs: /th/ *th*; Verbs: *think, throw*

Phonics Objectives

Can students:

✓ listen for the /th/ sound?

✓ identify the /th/ sound formed by the letter combination *th*?

✓ read and write words and sentences with the /th/ sound?

Language Acquisition Objectives

Can students:

✓ use the verbs *think, throw*?

ESL Standards

- Goal 2, Standard 2

Focusing on Phonemic Awareness

Say the word *thumb*, indicating your thumb, and stress the /th/ sound. Have students repeat the word *thumb*. Since /th/ is a difficult sound for some speakers, you might show students how to place the tongue between the teeth as you pronounce this sound. Now have the students repeat the word *think* after you. Exaggerate the *th* sound as you pronounce *think*. Ask the class to listen carefully as you say the following words; if a word has the /th/ sound they should raise their hands: *thick, ten, thin, bat, bath, bag, throw, thumb, Tom, mat, math, mitt, month, tree, three.*

Using Page 62

Ask students to:

- point to the letters *th*
- locate the words as you say them
- read aloud and track words with you

Point out *three months* on the page and display a calendar. Read aloud the months and the days of the week on the calendar and point out that Thursday begins with the /th/ sound. Show how the third, thirteenth, and thirtieth days of a month begin with the /th/ sound.

Activities for All Learners

Bingo Game
(Kinesthetic Learners)

Materials: cards or paper divided into grids—5 squares x 5 squares each, pens, pieces of torn paper (chits) to cover squares

Directions: Explain that students are going to play bingo. Briefly explain the rules (caller names square locations; players cover squares; the first person with a full line on his/her card wins). Have students (1) write the letters *B-I-N-G-O* in the squares across the top; (2) write random numbers between 1 and 10 under *B* and *I* (*not* in sequence), between 21 and 30 under *N* and *G*; and between 31 and 40 under *O*. Make small cards for the caller with each letter–number possibility (*B–3. B–8*) Note: This is a good game for practicing numbers.

Say It!

Teach the class the following chant:

Group 1: He's my friend through thick and thin.
Group 2: Thick and thin, thick and thin.
Group 1: He's my friend through thick and thin.
Group 2: He'll always be my friend.

Distribute copies of the chant on p. 99. Repeat the chant, substituting *She* for *He*. What does the term "through thick and thin" mean? Have students underline words containing the /th/ sound.

Write It!
Dictation

Ask students to study the sentences on p. 62 for homework. Dictate the sentences in random order. Have students underline words with the /th/ sound in them. Exchange papers and correct the dictations together.

Digraphs: /th/ *th* (voiceless)
New Word: with

th A Picnic *with* the Phonics Team

Write the word that finishes each sentence.

1. Will plays a game of _____baseball_____ *with* Mike.

2. Pat fishes in the _____ *with* Joe.

3. Tom dashes on the _____ *with* Jen.

4. Luz sits *with* Steve and plays a _____.

5. May is on the grass *with* the _____.

6. Bud runs away *with* Will's _____.

7. The van is by the grass *with* the _____.

8. A _____ jumps and makes a splash *with* its tail.

BUILDING BACKGROUND

Say the word *with,* stressing the /th/ sound and ask students to repeat it after you. Tell students that when you use *with* for people or things, it means the people or things are together. Ask a volunteer to stand next to you and say, (*student's name*) is *with* me. Ask students to get into pairs and say whom they are *with.* Then give directions to students using the word *with,* such as Go *with* (*student's name*) to the board. Discuss other ways students can use *with* in phrases, such as *coffee with milk.*

USING PAGE 63

Ask students to:
• point to the letters *th*
• locate the words as you say them
• read aloud and track words with you

Ask students to look at the scene on p. 63. Who is in the scene? What is happening? Read the title, "A Picnic *with* the Phonics Team" and point out the /th/ sound in the word *with.* Then ask students for examples of sentences using *with,* such as *I am with him* or *Come with me.*

ACTIVITIES FOR ALL LEARNERS

Descriptions *with* Picture Cards
(Visual Learners)

Materials: picture cards or pictures with scenes of people

Directions: Display picture cards of people, scenes, and activities along the chalk tray. Call on a volunteer and say, for example, *Point to the girl with the hat.* After the student indicates the correct picture, ask that student to say, *Point to . . .* for another student. Continue until all students have had a turn describing a picture. Encourage them to use the word *with* in their descriptions.

Read It!

Play the audiocassette of p. 63. Have students (1) read along and listen to the following lines and (2) repeat them as directed. Check pronunciation of the word *with* carefully.

1. Will plays a game of baseball *with* Mike.
2. Pat fishes in the lake *with* Joe.
3. Tom dashes on the sand *with* Jen.
4. Luz sits *with* Steve and plays a flute.
5. May is on the grass *with* the baby.
6. Bud runs away *with* Will's ball.
7. The van is by the grass *with* the shoes.
8. A fish jumps and makes a splash *with* its tail.

Write It!

 Ask students to write a one-page journal of their weekly routines. Suggest that they answer the following questions as they write:

• Do you live *with* your family?
• Do you walk or ride *with* anyone to school?
• Do you talk *with* people at school?
• Do you go out *with* friends on weekends?

Digraphs: /th/ *th* (voiced)
New Words: this, that

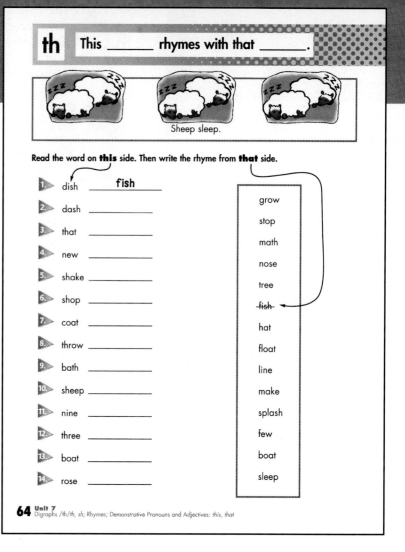

th — This _____ rhymes with that _____.

Sheep sleep.

Read the word on **this** side. Then write the rhyme from **that** side.

1. dish — fish
2. dash _____
3. that _____
4. new _____
5. shake _____
6. shop _____
7. coat _____
8. throw _____
9. bath _____
10. sheep _____
11. nine _____
12. three _____
13. boat _____
14. rose _____

grow
stop
math
nose
tree
~~fish~~
hat
float
line
make
splash
few
boat
sleep

64 Unit 7
Digraphs /th/*th, sh;* Rhymes; Demonstrative Pronouns and Adjectives: *this, that*

Phonics Objectives

Can students:
✓ listen for the /th/ sound?
✓ identify the /th/ sound formed by the letter combination *th*?
✓ read and write words and sentences with the /th/ sound?

Language Acquisition Objectives

Students:
• use rhyming words
• use the demonstrative pronouns and adjectives *this* and *that*

ESL Standards

• Goal 2, Standard 3

FOCUSING ON PHONEMIC AWARENESS

Say the words *this* and *thick*, stressing the /th/ and /th/ sounds. Point out that both words begin with the same *th* letters, but the letters make two different sounds. Compare the voiced /th/ sound in *this* with the unvoiced /th/ sound in *thick*. Explain that to make the /th/ sound, you place your tongue tip between your teeth before pronouncing the sound. Model the /th/ sound, blending it into the words *this* and *that*. Ask students to repeat the words after you.

USING PAGE 64

Ask students to:
• point to the letters *th*
• locate the words as you say them
• read aloud and track words with you

Read the title of the page aloud, "This . . . rhymes with that . . ." stressing the

/th/ sound. We say *this* for things that are near and *that* for things that are far away. They are words indicating location. Point to two examples: *This desk is my desk. That desk is his desk.* Explain that *this* and *that* can be either demonstrative pronouns or demonstrative adjectives. When used alone, *this* is a pronoun. Example: *This is a pen.* When used with a noun, *this* is an adjective. Example: *This pen is blue.* Point out how *this* and *that* are used on the page.

ACTIVITIES FOR ALL LEARNERS

Make This Puzzle
(Kinesthetic/Visual Learners)

Materials: A picture puzzle with many pieces—e.g., a map puzzle of the United States or an elaborate scene

Directions: Challenge a small group of students to assemble the puzzle in a given time. Explain that they must discuss the

pieces, using the word *this* and *that*. Examples: *Where does this piece go? Pass me that piece.* After they finish, invite them to explain how they did it. What strategy did they use to assemble this puzzle?

Sing a Rhyming Song
"Deep in the Heart of Texas" 🎧

🎵 Play the audiocassette of "Deep in the Heart of Texas." Distribute copies of the lyrics on p. 99 and invite students to underline the rhyming words. (*night/bright, sky/high, bloom/perfume, of/love*)

Write It!

✏️ Invite students to make up humorous verses or songs by using the rhyming words on p. 64. (*My love is like a red, red rose/Especially with her red, red nose . . .*) You may read examples of comical verse by poets like Ogden Nash or ask students to bring in favorite humorous poems or songs.

Review Words and New Words: bath, Beth, Roth, thumb, bathtub, three, thirty, throw, this, with, phone, wash, fish, she, splash, shake, sure

Phonics Objectives

Can students:
- ✓ listen for the digraph sounds /sh/, /f/, and /th/?
- ✓ read words with the digraphs *sh, ph,* and *th* in the context of a story?
- ✓ write words with *sh, ph, th*?

Language Acquisition Objectives

Can students:
- ✓ read words in story context?

Students:
- use the prepositions *with, to, at, in, on, till*

ESL Standards
- Goal 1, Standard 2

FOCUSING ON PHONEMIC AWARENESS

Song: "Splash, Splash" 🎵

🎵 Play the audiocassette of the song below. Distribute copies of the lyrics on p. 99.

Hey, May, can you baby-sit today?
I'll be there at three o'clock.
Three o'clock?
Splash, splash, give the baby a bath.
Let her play in the tub-tub-tub. Yeah!
Wash her ears and wash her nose.
Wash her fingers and wash her toes.
Splash, splash, time to get out of the bath.
I have to get that telephone!

USING THE AUDIOCASSETTE 🎧

Play the song again and invite students to sing along. Ask them to underline the words with the /sh/, /th/, and /ph/ sounds.

USING THE PHOTO PLAY

🎧 **Preview** the photo story, "Bath Time for Baby," with your students. Allow students time to look through the story and examine the pictures and text. Ask students to follow along as you play the audiocassette. They may wish to track the words as the play is read.

Background discussion: Ask students if they have ever baby-sat for family or friends. Have they ever had to help bathe a baby? What safety measures must a baby-sitter take when caring for small children?

Read the photo story together. Assign volunteers to read the parts of Mrs. Roth, May, Baby Beth, Will, and the narrator. As students read, listen for correct pronunciation of the *th, ph,* and *sh* sounds. Do not interrupt the story, but discuss problem words and errors in pronunciation after the reading. Model the correct pronunciations for students and ask them to repeat the words after you.

Review the play. Lead the class in a second reading of "Bath Time for Baby." This time, ask new volunteers to read the parts. After they finish reading, ask questions focusing on the content of the story:

- What is the name of the baby? (*Beth*)
- What is the name of the baby's mother? (*Mrs. Roth*)
- Who is the baby-sitter? (*May*)
- What time does May come to the Roth home? (*three o'clock*)
- What does the baby play with in the bathtub? (*a little fish*)
- Who phones May? (*Will*)
- Why can't May go to the movies? (*She has to baby-sit till nine o'clock.*)
- What does May give Baby Beth after the bath? (*a snack*)
- What does the baby do at last? (*She sleeps.*)

Challenge students to look back through the story and copy down all the words that have the /sh/, /th/, /th/, and /f/ sounds in them.

Questions

Digraphs: /sh/, *ph*, /th/

Review Words: think, phone, fish, bathtub, shakes, movies, Beth, splash, Roth, wash, throws

Phonics Objectives

Can students:
- ✓ listen for /sh/ as in *she*, /f/ as in *phone*, and /th/ as in *think*?
- ✓ identify the sounds the letters *sh*, *ph*, and *th* stand for?
- ✓ read words with the letters *sh*, *ph*, and *th* in sentences?

Language Acquisition Objectives

Can students:
- ✓ read and comprehend familiar words in a new context?
- ✓ deduce what word is needed to complete a sentence?

ESL Standards

- Goal 2, Standard 1

Questions

~~thinks~~	shakes
phone	movies
fish	Beth
bathtub	wash
Roth	throws

Complete the sentences below using a word from the box.

1. May _____**thinks**_____ this job is fun.

2. May says, "Okay, Baby Beth. Let's _____ your little thumbs and toes."

3. Mrs. _____ is the baby's mom.

4. The baby plays with a little _____.

5. The baby's name is _____.

6. She _____ the fish on the floor.

7. The baby _____ the phone and tries to eat it.

8. Baby Beth sits in the _____ and splashes.

9. Will says, "Do you want to go to the _____ with Mike and me?"

10. May says, "Don't eat the _____, Baby Beth!"

To discuss:
- Do you baby-sit?
- Do you have a job?
- Do you go to the movies? Name the movies you like.

66 Unit 7
Digraphs: *sh, ph, th*

BUILDING BACKGROUND

Ask students what is happening in the picture at the top of p. 66. Ask if anyone can retell the story on the previous page without turning back to look. Review the events of the photo story together.

USING PAGE 66

Review the list of words in the box at the top of p. 66. Read the instructions to the students. Have a student read the example. Point out that the word that completes the sentence (*thinks*) has been crossed out in the word box. Ask students to complete the remaining sentences on their own, crossing out the words in the box as they use them. Remind students they can turn back and reread the story if they need to check an answer. Encourage students to skim the text, looking for key words. Exchange books and go over answers together as a class.

Write It!
Dictation

Have students study the completed sentences on p. 66 for homework. Then dictate the sentences in reverse order, starting with sentence 10. Have students exchange papers and check their answers by referring to the completed sentences on p. 66. Note: This activity also serves as an assessment. You may note which sounds are causing difficulty for students through their misspellings.

ACTIVITIES FOR ALL LEARNERS

Change the Story
(Auditory Learners)

Materials: note paper, pens

Directions: Brainstorm possible changes to the story "Bath Time for Baby" with students (no phone call? two babies? an accident? a UFO?). Encourage students to be creative. Have them list suggestions and decide which ones they would like to

incorporate in a revised story. Have them rewrite the story with these changes. When you are finished, invite students to read their new stories aloud.

CONTENT LINKS

MATH and SCIENCE

/f/ /th/
Algebra by Allan Bellman et al.: Prentice Hall, 1998

/f/ /th/ /sh/
Physics: Problems and Principles by Paul Zitzewitz: Merrill Publishing Co., 1990

/th/ /f/
Earth and Physical Science by Mary Ann Christison: Addison Wesley Publishing Co., 1992

Achieving Competence in Science by Paul Cohen: Amsco School Publications Inc., 1993

Digraphs: sh, ph, th

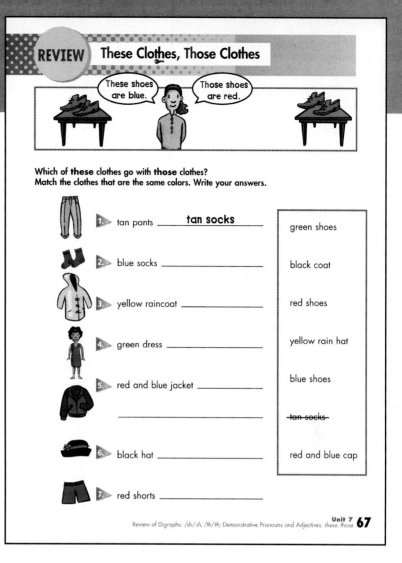

REVIEW These Clothes, Those Clothes

These shoes are blue.

Those shoes are red.

Which of these clothes go with those clothes?
Match the clothes that are the same colors. Write your answers.

1. tan pants _____tan socks_____
2. blue socks _____
3. yellow raincoat _____
4. green dress _____
5. red and blue jacket _____

_____

6. black hat _____
7. red shorts _____

green shoes

black coat

red shoes

yellow rain hat

blue shoes

~~tan socks~~

red and blue cap

Review of Digraphs: /sh/ sh, /th/ th; Demonstrative Pronouns and Adjectives: these, those **Unit 7 67**

Phonics Objectives

Can students:
✔ listen for and identify the /sh/ and /th/ sounds formed by letter combinations *sh* and *th*?
✔ read and write words with the /sh/ and /th/ sounds?

Language Acquisition Objectives

Can students:
✔ use the demonstrative pronouns and adjectives *these* and *those*?
✔ use singular and plural?

ESL Standards

• Goal 2, Standard 1

BUILDING BACKGROUND

Take several pens in your hand. Say, *These are pens.* Then point to some pencils at a distance on another desk and say, *Those are pencils.* Hand the pens to a student and ask him/her to say, *These are pens.* Then ask the student to point to the pencils and say, *Those are pencils.* Write *this* and *that* on the board. Explain that these words are singular demonstrative pronouns. They take the place of singular nouns. Write *these* and *those* on the board and explain that these words are plural demonstrative pronouns, which take the place of plural nouns. Point out that *this, that, these,* and *those* can also function as demonstrative adjectives.

USING THE REVIEW PAGE

Ask students to:
• point to the letters *th*
• locate the words as you say them
• read aloud and track words with you

Read the title of the page aloud. Explain how *these* and *those* are used in the box. Point out that *th* is not pronounced in the word *clothes.* Discuss the clothes students are wearing and review colors. Then explain that they will match clothes according to color, using *this, that, these,* and *those* as adjectives.

ACTIVITIES FOR ALL LEARNERS

This and These Pictures
(Kinesthetic/Auditory Learners)

Materials: picture cards or pictures of single items and groups of items

Directions: Place pictures of single items and multiple items, such as one car or two trees, along the chalk rail. Ask a volunteer to point to a picture and use the term *this/these* or *that/those.* (Example: *That is a dog. Those are hats.*) Continue with more volunteers.

Say It!

Teach the class the following chant:

Group 1: What's this? What's this?
Group 2: It's a shirt. It's a shirt.
Group 1: What's that? What's that?
Group 2: It's a skirt. It's a skirt.
Group 1: What are these? What are these?
Group 2: They're my shoes. They're my shoes.
Group 1: What are those? What are those?
Group 2: Oh, those? Who knows?

Distribute copies of the chant on p. 99. Have students repeat the chant, alternating parts. Have students underline words containing the /th/ and /sh/ sounds.

Write It!

Write *this* and *these* on the board. Then write the following sentences with blanks. Ask a student to read the sentences and fill in the blanks with *this* or *these.* Ask students to write 10 similar sentences of their own.

I want to read _____ book. (*this/these*)
(*This/These*) _____ plants are wet.

UNIT 8

Digraphs: wh, ng, ch, tch, wr, kn

Digraphs: /hw/ wh

New Words: what, white, whale, wheel, whistle, wheat

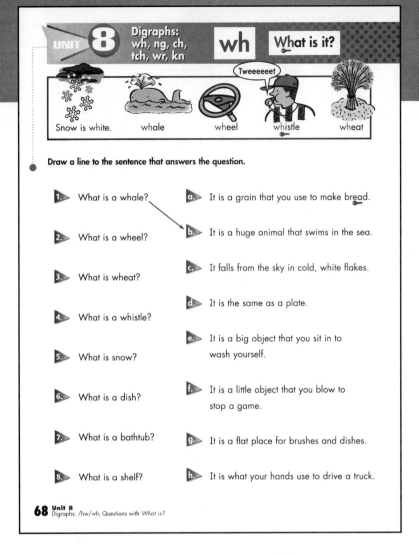

Phonics Objectives

Can students:
- ✓ listen for the /hw/ sound?
- ✓ identify the /hw/ sound formed by the letter combination *wh*?
- ✓ read and write words and sentences with the /hw/ sound?

Language Acquisition Objectives

Can students:
- ✓ use the question word *what*?

ESL Standards
- Goal 2, Standard 1

FOCUSING ON PHONEMIC AWARENESS

Explain that the words at the top of p. 68 begin with the letters *wh*, which stand for the /hw/ sound. The /h/ sound comes before the /w/ sound. Have students hold their finger to their mouths and repeat these words after you: *white, whale, wheel*. Ask, *Do you feel your breath on your finger as you say the /hw/ sound?* Invite students to say *whistle* and *wheat*. Ask students to listen as you say the following words and raise their hands if it begins with the /hw/ sound: <u>white</u>, *wide, wet, water,* <u>what</u>, *walk,* <u>wheat</u>, *window,* <u>whale</u>, *wash, wind, with,* <u>wheel</u>.

USING PAGE 68

Ask students to:
- point to the letters *wh*
- locate the words as you say them
- read aloud and track words with you

Read the title of the page, "What is it?," stressing the /hw/. Explain that the five question words in English that start with the letters *wh* (/hw/ sound) are *what, where, when, why, who.*

ACTIVITIES FOR ALL LEARNERS

What Is It? Guess the Picture
(Kinesthetic/Visual Learners)

Materials: picture cards or pictures of common items

Directions: Divide students into pairs. Give each a set of 10 picture cards, face down. Explain that partners will take turns. One will draw a card and describe it and the other will guess what is pictured on the card. (Example: *It has four legs. It can live in a house. It barks. What is it?*) Partners alternate picking cards and guessing until all cards are gone. They can exchange cards when finished.

Read it! 🎧

Play the audiocassette of p. 68. Have students (1) read along and listen to the following lines and (2) repeat them as directed. Check pronunciation of the *wh* words carefully.

Snow is white. whale wheel whistle wheat
1. What is a whale? It is a huge animal that swims in the sea.
2. What is a wheel? It is what your hands use to drive a truck.
3. What is wheat? It is a grain that you use to make bread.
4. What is a whistle? It is a little object that you blow to stop a game.
5. What is snow? It falls from the sky in cold, white flakes.
6. What is a dish? It is the same as a plate.
7. What is a bathtub? It is a big object that you sit in to wash yourself.
8. What is a shelf? It is a flat place for brushes and dishes.

Write It!

 Ask students to underline words with the digraphs *wh, sh,* or *th.*

Digraphs: /hw/ *wh*

New Words: when, one, two, three, four, five, six, seven, eight, nine, ten, eleven, twelve, thirteen, fourteen, fifteen, sixteen, seventeen, eighteen, nineteen, twenty, twenty-one, twenty-two, twenty-three, twenty-four, twenty-five, twenty-six, twenty-seven, twenty-eight, twenty-nine, thirty, forty, fifty, sixty

Phonics Objectives

Can students:
- ✓ listen for the /hw/ sound?
- ✓ identify the /hw/ sound formed by the letter combination *wh*?
- ✓ read and write words and sentences with the /hw/ sound?

Language Acquisition Objectives

Can students:
- ✓ use the question word *when*?
- ✓ use the numbers 1–60?
- ✓ tell time using the numbers 1–60?

ESL Standards

- Goal 1, Standard 2

FOCUSING ON PHONEMIC AWARENESS

Say *when* for the class, stressing the initial /hw/ sound. Ask the class to repeat it. Model the /hw/ sound by saying the /h/ and then the /w/. Then explain that the word *when* is used to inquire about time.

Display a large clock. Ask students, *When do you wake up?* Invite a volunteer to position the hands on the clock to show the time he/she wakes up. Ask other *when* questions, inviting students to answer by positioning the hands on the clock. (Examples: *When does school end? When do you eat lunch?*)

USING PAGE 69

Ask students to:
- point to the letters *wh*
- locate the words as you say them
- read aloud and track words with you

Point out the title of the page, "When?", and explain that students will learn about numbers and telling time on this page. Teach the numbers in the box. Then show various times on the clock, asking students to interpret the time.

ACTIVITIES FOR ALL LEARNERS

Clap on Five: Numbers game
(Kinesthetic/Auditory Learners)

Directions: Explain that students will play a game called "Clap on Five." Whenever they hear the word *five* or a multiple of five they should clap. Ask them to count with you slowly as you demonstrate: 1, 2, 3, 4, *clap*, 6, 7, 8, 9, *clap*, 11, 12, 13, 14, *clap*. Point to the first person in the first row and ask that person to say *one*, the second person to say *two*, etc. Continue down the rows until you reach *five*. Be sure that person claps instead of saying *five*. Have students continue counting and clapping on *fives* and multiples of five.

Say It! 🎧

Teach the class the following chant:

Group 1: What time is it? What time is it?
Group 2: It's seven o'clock. It's time for the bus.
Group 1: What time is it? What time is it?
Group 2: It's eight o'clock. Don't wait for us.

Distribute copies of the chant on p. 100. Repeat the chant and ask the groups to exchange parts.

Write It!

Dictate the following questions and answers. Ask students to complete each answer with their own times.

1. When do you get up? I get up at _____.
2. When do you go to class? I go to class at _____.
3. When do you eat lunch? I eat lunch at _____.
4. When do you go to sleep? I go to sleep at _____.

---

wh	When?

1	2	3	4	5	6	7	8	9	10
one	two	three	four	five	six	seven	eight	nine	ten
11	12	13	14	15	16	17	18		
eleven	twelve	thirteen	fourteen	fifteen	sixteen	seventeen	eighteen		
19	20	21	22	23	24	25			
nineteen	twenty	twenty-one	twenty-two	twenty-three	twenty-four	twenty-five			
26	27	28	29	30	40	50	60		
twenty-six	twenty-seven	twenty-eight	twenty-nine	thirty	forty	fifty	sixty		

Write the time in numbers. Then write the words from the box above that stand for your numbers.

1. ▶ When do you wake up? I wake up at **6:30** _(numbers)_ **six thirty** _(words)_.

2. ▶ When do you wash your face? I wash at _____ _____.

3. ▶ When do you go to class? I go to class at _____ _____.

4. ▶ When do you have a snack? I have a snack at _____ _____.

5. ▶ When is your last class? My last class is at _____ _____.

6. ▶ When do you go back home? I go home at _____ _____.

7. ▶ When do you study? I study at _____ _____.

8. ▶ When do you go to bed? I go to bed at _____ _____.

Digraphs: /hw/wh; Questions with *When?* **Unit 8 69**

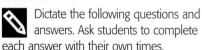

Digraphs: /ng/ *ng*

New Words: sing, song, king, ring, long, string, hungry

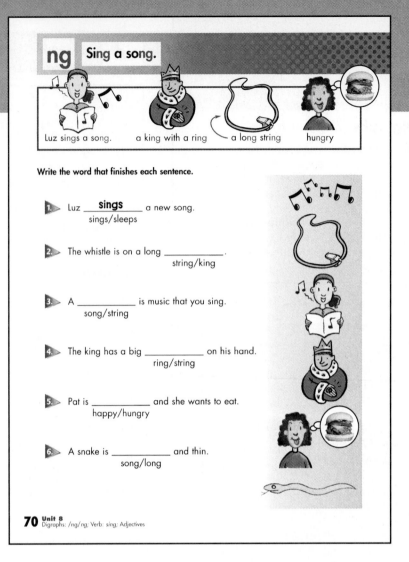

ng Sing a song.

Luz sings a song. a king with a ring a long string hungry

Write the word that finishes each sentence.

1. Luz __sings__ a new song.
   sings/sleeps

2. The whistle is on a long _____.
   string/king

3. A _____ is music that you sing.
   song/string

4. The king has a big _____ on his hand.
   ring/string

5. Pat is _____ and she wants to eat.
   happy/hungry

6. A snake is _____ and thin.
   song/long

70 Unit 8
Digraphs: /ng/*ng*; Verb: *sing*; Adjectives

FOCUSING ON PHONEMIC AWARENESS

Say the word *ring*, stressing the /ng/ sound. Ask students to say it with you. Explain that some words in English end with the /ng/ sound as in *ring*. Show students how to make this sound by lifting the back of the tongue to the roof of their mouths. This is a nasal sound that students may not know. Let them practice making the /ng/ sound a few times. Ask the class to listen carefully as you say the following words and raise their hands if they hear the /ng/ sound: *sun, song, king, can, sing, swim, line, long, step, string, home, hungry.*

USING PAGE 70

Ask students to:
- point to the letters *ng*
- locate the words as you say them
- read aloud and track words with you

Read aloud the title of the page, "Sing a song," stressing the /ng/ sounds. Explain that *sing* is a verb. Demonstrate by singing *la, la, la.* Review songs that they have learned.

ACTIVITIES FOR ALL LEARNERS

Top Ten Songs
(Visual /Auditory Learners)

Materials: Paper, pens

Directions: (1) Tell students to write their names on a piece of paper; (2) ask them to turn the paper over and write the title "Top Ten Favorite Songs" on the paper and list ten of their favorite songs. (The songs can be in languages other than English.) Post the lists and invite students to guess who wrote each list. Encourage discussion of musical preferences and music in different cultures.

Song: "Long, Long Trail"
(Auditory Learners)

Play the audiocassette of "Long, Long Trail." Distribute copies of the lyrics on p. 100 and invite students to underline the /ng/ words. (*long, winding, nightingales, singing, waiting, going*)

Write It!

Read the following incomplete rhymes and ask students to write the word from p. 70 that completes each.

1. You can't go wrong if you sing a _____. (*song*)
2. The hand of the king has a gold _____. (*ring*)
3. My favorite thing is to dance and _____. (*sing*)
4. On her neck she wears a ring hanging from a _____. (*string*)

Can students make up more rhymes using other words they have learned? Brainstorm rhymes as a class and write them on the board.

Digraphs: /ng/ -ing
New Word: thinking

-ing   Pat is thinking.

$2a + 4a = 3b$
$a = ?$

She is thinking. = She thinks.

Write the letter that matches the sentence.

1. Luz is singing a song.   **h**
2. Steve is reading.   ____
3. Jen is washing the dishes.   ____
4. Will is swimming.   ____
5. Mike is riding a bike.   ____
6. Steve is sleeping.   ____
7. Bud is eating the meat.   ____
8. The frog is jumping.   ____
9. May is taking a plate.   ____
10. Tom is jogging.   ____

a   b   c   d   e   f   g   h   i   j

Digraphs: /ng/ng; Present Progressive Verbs   **Unit 8 71**

BUILDING BACKGROUND

On the chalkboard, write the word *think* and read it aloud. What kind of word or part of speech is *think*? (*a verb*) Add -*ing* to *think*, forming the word *thinking*. Explain that the ending -*ing* can be added to verbs to show that the action is happening right now. Explain that this verb ending indicates an ongoing action in the present. Ask the class to listen as you say these action words and repeat each word, adding an -*ing* ending: *sing, wash, jump, read, sleep, eat.* (Example: *think—thinking.*)

USING PAGE 71

Ask students to:
• point to the letters -*ing*
• locate the words as you say them
• read aloud and track words with you

Read the two sentences in the box on the page. Contrast the sentence *She is thinking.* (now), with the sentence *She thinks.* (every day). Point out the difference between the present progressive tense

(an action happening now) and the simple present tense (an action that happens in general). The present progressive tense does not exist in all languages and may be a new concept for some students.

Then point out that some action words change before the -*ing* ending is added. Write *swim* and *swimming* on the board. Point out that an extra *m* was added before -*ing*. Write the words *ride* and *riding* and explain how the final *e* in *ride* was dropped before -*ing* was added. Let students practice changing the last letter of the words *take, make, run, hit,* and *jog* as they add -*ing* endings.

ACTIVITIES FOR ALL LEARNERS

Playing Charades
(Kinesthetic Learners)

Invite students to play charades in teams using verbs they have learned. Ask students to guess the verbs using the -*ing* form—i.e. *singing, jogging,* etc.

Read It! 🎧

Play the audiocassette of p. 71. Have students (1) read along and listen to the following lines and (2) repeat them as directed. Check pronunciation of the /ng/ words carefully.

She is thinking. She thinks.
1. Luz is singing a song.
2. Steve is reading.
3. Jen is washing the dishes.
4. Will is swimming.
5. Mike is riding a bike.
6. Steve is sleeping.
7. Bud is eating the meat.
8. The frog is jumping.
9. May is taking a plate.
10. Tom is jogging.

Write It!

Ask the class to listen as you say some action words and to write the words with -*ing* endings: *wash, eat, read, jump, sleep, sing.* Review the work as a class.

Digraphs: /ch/ *ch*

New Words: cheese, lunch, sandwich, lunchbox, chicken, peach, check

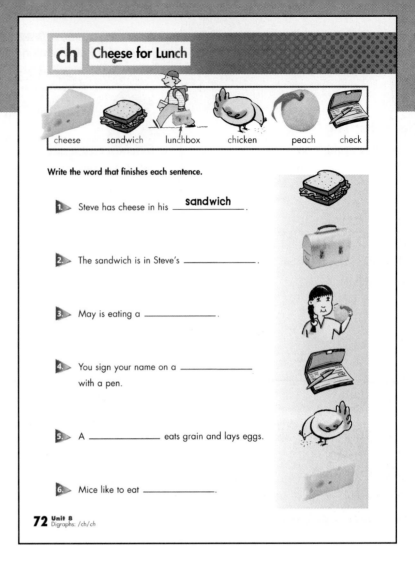

ch | Cheese for Lunch

cheese   sandwich   lunchbox   chicken   peach   check

Write the word that finishes each sentence.

1. Steve has cheese in his __sandwich__ .

2. The sandwich is in Steve's _____ .

3. May is eating a _____ .

4. You sign your name on a _____ with a pen.

5. A _____ eats grain and lays eggs.

6. Mice like to eat _____ .

72 Unit 8
Digraphs: /ch/*ch*

FOCUSING ON PHONEMIC AWARENESS

Say the word *lunch*. Point out that the letters *ch* work together to stand for the /ch/ sound. Model this sound by pushing out your lips slightly, putting your teeth together, and pushing the air out with your tongue as you say the /ch/ sound. Let students mimic your actions. Say *lunch* again and invite the class to repeat it after you. Ask students to listen as you say some words with the /ch/ sound, repeat each word, then tell you if the /ch/ sound is heard at the beginning, middle, or end of the word. Use the following words: *cheese, peach, sandwich, lunchbox, check, chicken, lunch.*

USING PAGE 72

Ask students to:
- point to the letters *ch*
- locate the words as you say them
- read aloud and track words with you

Point out the words *cheese, sandwich, chicken,* and *peach* on the page and read them aloud. Ask what these words have in common besides the /ch/ sound. (They are things that you can eat.)

ACTIVITIES FOR ALL LEARNERS

Make Menus
(Visual Learners)

Materials: drawing paper and markers or computer clip art, sample menus

Directions: Divide students into pairs or small groups. Ask them to make menus, including at least three *ch* words. Encourage them to illustrate their menus. They may use drawings or, if a computer lab is available, they can print out typed menus and add computer clip art. Display the menus and discuss them.

Write a Check
(Kinesthetic/Visual Learners)

Materials: checkbook, checks, pens

Directions: Bring in sample checks from a local bank, distribute them, and explain to students how they are used. (Since checks are not used routinely in all countries, these may be new to some students.) Sketch a large check on the board or make an overhead transparency. Guide students in filling out the check line by line.

Say It!

 Teach the class the following chant:

Group 1: A chicken wing, an onion ring,
Group 2: A slice of cheese to munch.
Group 1: A peach or two, a bowl of stew,
Group 2: Now that's a tasty lunch!

Distribute copies of the chant on p. 100. Have students underline words containing the /ch/ sound.

Write It!

Ask students to write the words from p. 72 that contain the *ch* sound and make sentences of their own using these words. Have them underline the *ch* words in each sentence.

Digraphs: /ch/ *tch*

New Words: catch, pitch, watch, scratch, match, crutches

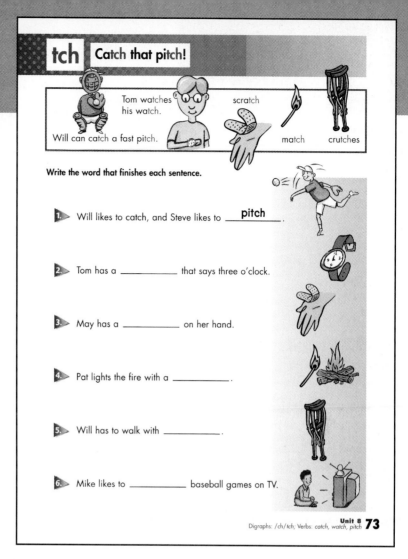

tch | **Catch that pitch!**

Tom watches his watch.   scratch   match   crutches
Will can catch a fast pitch.

Write the word that finishes each sentence.

1. Will likes to catch, and Steve likes to ___**pitch**___.

2. Tom has a _____ that says three o'clock.

3. May has a _____ on her hand.

4. Pat lights the fire with a _____.

5. Will has to walk with _____.

6. Mike likes to _____ baseball games on TV.

FOCUSING ON PHONEMIC AWARENESS

Say *pitch* and *catch* and have the class repeat these words. Ask, *What sound do both of these words have in common?* (the /ch/ sound, the letters *tch*) Explain that in English, the letters *tch* stand for the /ch/ sound. Say the word *catch* and model oral blending: *caaaaatch*. Remind students that the letters *ch* also stand for the /ch/ sound as in the word *lunch*.

Tell students to listen carefully as you say the following words and raise their hands if they hear the /ch/ sound: cat, *catch*, sky, *scratch*, mats, *match*, *watch*, walk.

USING PAGE 73

Ask students to:
- point to the letters *tch*
- locate the words as you say them
- read aloud and track words with you

Explain that the word *watch* can be either a verb or noun. To illustrate this, point out the sentence at the top of the page: *Tom watches his watch.* Read the sentence aloud to the class and ask which *watch* is an action word and which *watch* is a noun. Point out that *pitch* and *catch* can also be nouns or verbs. Do students know any other words that function as both a noun and a verb? (*check, scratch, match*)

ACTIVITIES FOR ALL LEARNERS

Watching TV
(Visual Learners)

Discuss favorite TV programs. Write categories of programs on the chalkboard, e.g., sports, news, sit-coms, documentaries. Ask students to poll their friends and family for their favorite TV programs and list the results. Post results for students to read and compare.

Read It! 🎧

Play the audiocassette of p. 73. Have students (1) read along and listen to the following lines and (2) repeat them as directed. Check pronunciation of the /ch/ words carefully.

Will can catch a fast pitch.
Tom watches his watch.
scratch match crutches

1. Will likes to catch, and Steve likes to pitch.
2. Tom has a watch that says three o'clock.
3. May has a scratch on her hand.
4. Pat lights the fire with a match.
5. Will has to walk with crutches.
6. Mike likes to watch baseball games on TV.

Write It!
Dictation

Have students study the completed sentences on p. 73 for homework. Then dictate the sentences in reverse order, starting with sentence 6. Ask students to underline words with the /ch/ sound in them.

Silent Letters: /r/ wr, /n/ kn

New Words: wrong, know, write, knee, knife

| | wr | Right or Wrong? | kn | Do you know? |

Circle *right* if the sentence is correct. Circle *wrong* if it is not correct.

1.	Students write on a desk.		(right)	wrong
2.	Your knee is near your face.		right	wrong
3.	Cats can write.		right	wrong
4.	Math problems make you think.		right	wrong
5.	229–120=209		right	wrong
6.	Monkeys read and know math.		right	wrong
7.	You can drink milk with a knife.		right	wrong
8.	You can make a sandwich with cheese in it.		right	wrong
9.	A peach is a fruit.		right	wrong
10.	Cats can make a scratch on your hand.		right	wrong
11.	A watch goes on your leg.		right	wrong
12.	You can catch a ball with a mitt.		right	wrong
13.	You can catch a fish with a match.		right	wrong
14.	You can cut a sandwich with a knife.		right	wrong

74 Unit 8
Digraphs, Silent Letters: /r/wr, /n/kn; Verbs: *write, know, think, catch*; Adjectives: *right, wrong*; Homonyms

FOCUSING ON PHONEMIC AWARENESS

Remind students that, in English, some words can have silent letters (like silent *e*). Point to your knee and say the word *knee*. What letter usually stands for the first sound you hear in the word *knee*? (*n*) Explain that the word *knee* starts with a silent *k*. Then point out that the letter *w* is silent when it is combined with *r*, as in *write*.

USING PAGE 74

Ask students to:
- point to the letters *wr, kn*
- locate the words as you say them
- read aloud and track words with you

Read the title sentences on p. 74 aloud. Point out the silent *w* in *wrong* and the silent *k* in *know*. Explain that *right* and *wrong* are opposite adjectives. Ask students, *Do you know that?* Review the

question form *Do you . . . .* Brainstorm questions that can begin with *Do you know*, such as *Do you know what . . . ?* and *Do you know how to . . . ?*

ACTIVITIES FOR ALL LEARNERS

Do you know . . . ?
(Auditory Learners)

Materials: index cards

Directions: Divide students into pairs. Ask each pair to write *where, how, when, who,* and *how* on index cards, turn the cards over, and mix them up. Explain that partners take turns picking cards and making questions that include the word on the card. (Examples: *Do you know <u>where</u> the office is? Do you know <u>when</u> school ends?*) Invite students to share their questions at the end.

Say It!: 🎧
Teach the class the following chant.

Group 1: She's never wrong.
Group 2: She's always right.
Group 1: She's perfect as can be.
Group 2: She knows it all.
Group 1: She's very bright.
Group 2: Almost as bright as me!

Distribute copies of the chant on p. 100. Have groups exchange parts and repeat the chant, substituting the pronoun *he* for *she*. Ask students to underline words containing the *wr* and *kn* sounds.

Write It!
A Quiz

Have students make up their own *right/wrong* quiz. Encourage them to have fun and make the sentences outrageous if they wish. (*You catch a pitch with crutches. right/wrong*) Suggest that they use words containing the /ch/, /tch/, /wh/, /ng/, /kn/, and /wr/ sounds. Photocopy the quizzes and distribute one each day for several weeks for students to enjoy.

Photo Play: "Going to the Doctor"

Review Words: what, where, when, knee, check, knife, know, catch, crutches, wrong

New Words: doctor, office, bend, X-ray, pain

Phonics Objectives

Can students:
- ✓ listen for the /hw/, /ng/, /ch/, /r/, and /n/ sounds?
- ✓ read words with the letter combinations *wh*, *ng*, *ch*, *tch*, *kn*, and *wr* in the context of a story?
- ✓ write words with the letter combinations *wh*, *ch*, *tch*, *ng*, *wr*, *kn*?

Language Acquisition Objectives

Can students:
- ✓ read words in story context?
- ✓ use question words?

ESL Standards
- Goal 1, Standard 2

Going to the Doctor

Scene: A doctor's office. The doctor is checking Will's knee.

Doctor: What is the problem, Will?

Will: I can't walk. I think the problem is in my right knee.

Doctor: Where is the pain? On the top of the knee or on the side?

Will: On the top *and* the side. It feels like a knife is in the knee.

Doctor: Let's see, Will. Can you bend the knee at all?

Will: No. See? It's huge and red.

Doctor: Yes, I see. It is badly swollen. We need to take an X-ray of this knee.

Will: An X-ray? Is it that bad?

Doctor: I don't know for sure, Will. The X-ray is like a photo of the knee. It will show where the problem is.

Will: When can I play baseball again? We have a game on Friday, and I have to catch.

Doctor: Sorry, Will. You may be on crutches this Friday.

Will: Crutches! What bad luck!

Doctor: Let's go take that X-ray. I may be wrong.

Unit 8 75
Digraphs: wh, ng, ch, tch, wr, kn

FOCUSING ON PHONEMIC AWARENESS

Song: "Bad Knee Blues" 🎧

🎵 Play the audiocassette of the song below. Distribute copies of the lyrics on p. 100.

I went to the doctor
To check out my knee.
"What's wrong?" said the doctor.
The pain is killing me.
The doctor said that I can't play
And now I need to get an X-ray.
When I bend down to catch the ball.
When I stand up and walk down the hall.
The doctor said that I can't play
And now I need to get an X-ray.

USING THE AUDIOCASSETTE 🎧

Play the song again and invite students to sing along. Ask them to underline words that contain the /ch/, /tch/, /wh/, /wr/, /ng/, and /kn/ sounds.

USING THE PHOTO PLAY

🎧 **Preview** the photo play, "Going to the Doctor," with your students. Allow students time to look through it and examine the picture and text. Ask students to follow along as you play the audiocassette. They may wish to track the words as the play is read.

Background discussion: Ask students if they have ever had an injury. Did they go to the doctor? Did they ever have an X-ray? Have they, or has someone they know, used crutches? What happened?

Read the photo play together. Assign volunteers to read the parts of the doctor and Will. As students read, listen for correct pronunciation of the *ch, tch, wh, wr, ng,* and *kn* sounds. Do not interrupt the story, but discuss problem words and errors in pronunciation after the reading. Model the correct pronunciations for students and ask them to repeat the words after you.

Review the story. Lead the class in a second reading of "Going to the Doctor." This time, ask new volunteers to read the parts. After they finish reading, ask questions focusing on the content of the story:

- Where is Will? (*in a doctor's office*)
- What is Will's problem? (*He can't walk. He has pain in his right knee.*)
- Where is the pain? (*on the top and side of the knee*)
- Can Will bend his right knee? (*no*)
- What does the doctor need to do? (*take an X-ray*)
- What game does Will want to play on Friday? (*baseball*)
- Why can't he play? (*He may be on crutches.*)

Challenge students to look back through the story and copy down all the words that have the /wh/, /ch/, /tch/, /ng/, /wr/, and /kn/ sounds in them. When they are finished, review the activity as a class.

Questions

Digraphs: /wh/, /ch/, /ng/, /r/, /n/

Review Words: what, where, when, knee, check, knife, know, catch, crutches, wrong

Phonics Objectives

Can students:
- ✓ listen for the digraphs /hw/, /ng/, /ch/, /r/, and /n/?
- ✓ identify the sounds the letters *wh*, *ng*, *tch*, *ch*, *wr*, and *kn* stand for?
- ✓ read words with the letters *wh*, *ng*, *ch*, *tch*, *wr*, and *kn* in sentences?

Language Acquisition Objectives

Can students:
- ✓ read and comprehend words in a new context?
- ✓ write a complete sentence to answer a question?

ESL Standards

- Goal 1, Standard 2

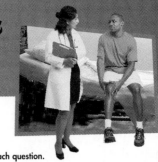

Questions

Write a complete sentence to answer each question.

1. Where is Will? **Will is at the doctor's office.**

2. What is Will's problem? _____

3. Where is Will's pain? _____

4. What does the pain feel like? _____

5. What is an X-ray? _____

6. When is Will's baseball game? _____

To discuss:
- Where do you go when you have a pain?
- When do you go to a doctor?
- Is your doctor a man or a woman?
- What can you do to help pain at home?

76 Unit 8
Digraphs, Question Words with /hw/: where, what, when

BUILDING BACKGROUND

Ask students what is happening in the picture at the top of p. 76. Ask if anyone can retell the story on the previous page without turning back to look. Review the events of the photo play together. Ask students if they have ever been to a female doctor. What can an X-ray show? What happens if a knee is injured seriously?

USING PAGE 76

Read the instructions to the students. Have a student read the sample question and answer. Remind students to write a complete sentence as they answer the remaining questions. They can turn back and reread the story if they need to check an answer. Encourage students to skim the text, looking for key words. Exchange books and go over answers together as a class. You may wish to use the discussion questions at the bottom of p. 76 for language enrichment. Invite students to explain their answers in detail.

Write a Journal

Invite students to brainstorm health issues, previous injuries, and trips to the doctor or hospital. Suggest that they write about their experiences in one or two paragraphs in their journals. What were their feelings? What sensory memories do they have? (sounds? smells? sights? tastes?) If students prefer not to write about themselves, they might write about someone they know.

ACTIVITIES FOR ALL LEARNERS

Calling 911
(Auditory Learners)

Materials: cell phone or paper phone, other props as needed

Directions: Explain to students that they are going to role-play an emergency scene, and someone will call 911 for help. Discuss what the emergencies might be. (*injury, accident, fire, crime*) Request volunteers for the various roles.

CONTENT LINKS

READING and LITERATURE
/ng/ /kn/
King Arthur and the Knights of the Round Table: Penguin Reader Series, 2000

/ng/
White Fang by Jack London: Penguin American Classics, 2000
Snow Falling on Cedars by David Guterson: Penguin Readers, 2000

/ch/ /tch/
The Chamber by John Grisham: Penguin Readers, 2000
The Witch of Blackbird Pond by Elizabeth George Speare: Yearling Books, 1978

/wh/
The Horse Whisperer by Nicholas Evans: Penguin Reader Series, 2000
The Woman in White by Wilkie Collins, Penguin Readers Collected Classics, 2000

Digraphs: *wh, ng, ch, tch, wr, kn*

Phonics Objectives

Can students:
✓ listen for the /hw/, /ng/, /ch/, /r/, and /n/ sounds?
✓ identify the /hw/, /ng/, /ch/, /r/, and /n/ sounds formed by different letter combinations?
✓ read and write words with the letter combinations *wh, ng, ch, tch, wr,* and *kn*?

Language Acquisition Objectives

Can students:
✓ use present progressive verbs?
✓ use rhyming words?

ESL Standards

• Goal 2, Standard 3

REVIEW   Words that Rhyme

dish	scratch	wheat	shine	king	dash
playing	knee	know	that	shake	sheep
glue	walking	write	when	hopping	song
bath	flying	snowing	thinking	these	taking

Write the rhyming word from the box on the line next to each word below.

1. fish _____ dish _____
2. then _____
3. cat _____
4. snake _____
5. ring _____
6. long _____
7. line _____
8. math _____
9. meat _____
10. white _____
11. blue _____
12. sleep _____
13. three _____
14. snow _____
15. splash _____
16. catch _____
17. talking _____
18. crying _____
19. stopping _____
20. blowing _____
21. saying _____
22. drinking _____
23. keys _____
24. making _____

Unit 8
Review of Digraphs; Rhymes **77**

BUILDING BACKGROUND

Write the following words on the chalkboard: *whale, king, lunch, match.* Ask the class, Which word ends with *ng*? (*king*) Begins with *wh*? (*whale*) Ends with *ch*? (*lunch*) Ends with *tch*? (*match*) Then write the words *know* and *wrong* on the board. Ask a volunteer to read the words aloud and circle the silent letters.

Review with the class that words with the same ending sound are called rhyming words. Ask students to think of words they know that rhyme. Write their examples on the board.

USING THE REVIEW PAGE

Ask students to:
• point to the letters *wh, ng, tch, wr, kn*
• locate the words as you say them
• read aloud with you and track words

Read aloud the title of the page, "Words that rhyme", and ask students to repeat it.

Review the exercise as a class or divide the class into pairs, have them complete the page together, and let them compare their answers.

ACTIVITIES FOR ALL LEARNERS

Rhyming Concentration
(**Kinesthetic/Visual Learners**)

Materials: index cards

Directions: Divide the class into pairs. Explain that students are going to play a rhyming card game. Have them copy the following words from the board onto an index card: *when, then, king, ring, know, throw, wheat, eat, catch, match, knee, three, fish, dish, cat, that, snake, shake, long, song, line, shine, math, bath, white, write, splash, dash.* Mix up the cards and place them facedown. Have players alternate turning over 2 cards and reading the words aloud. If the 2 words rhyme, the player keeps the cards. The player with the most cards at the end of the game wins.

Read It! 🎧

Play the audiocassette of p. 77. Have students (1) read along and listen to the following lines and (2) repeat them as directed. Check pronunciation of the rhyming words carefully.

1. fish/dish
2. then/when
3. cat/that
4. snake/shake
5. ring/king
6. long/song
7. line/shine
8. math/bath
9. meat/wheat
10. white/write
11. blue/glue
12. sleep/sheep
13. three/knee
14. snow/know
15. splash/dash
16. catch/scratch
17. talking/walking
18. crying/flying
19. stopping/hopping
20. blowing/snowing
21. saying/playing
22. drinking/thinking
23. keys/these
24. making/taking

Write It!

For a homework assignment, ask students to write 20 sentences using words from the box on p. 77.

---

r-Controlled Vowels: /är/ ar

New Words: start, car, charge, card, farm, barn, garden, star, dark, arm, part

Phonics Objectives

Can students:
- ✓ listen for the /är/ sound?
- ✓ identify the /är/ sound formed by the letter combination *ar*?
- ✓ read and write words and sentences with the /är/ sound?

Language Acquisition Objectives

Can students:
- ✓ use the verbs *are*, *start*?
- ✓ use farm words: *barn*, *farm*, *garden*?
- ✓ use transportation words: *car*, *start*?
- ✓ use shopping words: *charge card*?

ESL Standards

- Goal 2, Standard 1
- Goal 3, Standard 3

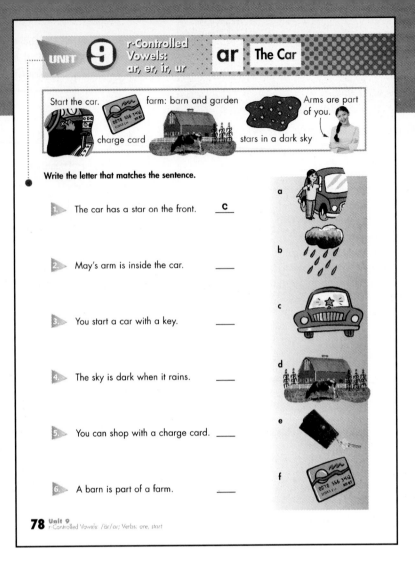

FOCUSING ON PHONEMIC AWARENESS

Explain that in English the letters *a* and *r* together often represent the /är/ sound. Indicate your arm and say the word *arm*, stressing the /är/ sound. Invite the class to repeat *arm* after you. Point out that when the letter *r* follows a vowel, the vowel sound sometimes changes. Remind students of the /o/ sound that they learned in the words *for*, *more*, *sports*, and *before*. Ask the class to listen carefully as you say the following words; if a word has the /är/ sound, they should raise their hands: *farm, fast, far, car, card, cap, goat, garden, desk, dark, boat, barn, stand, star, start, charge, check.*

USING PAGE 78

Ask students to:
- point to the letters *ar*
- locate the words as you say them
- read aloud and track words with you

Point out the sentence *Start the car* at the top of p. 78. Explain that the verb *start* is the opposite of *stop*. Point out the sentence *Arms are part of you.* Explain that, while *am* and *is* are singular forms of the verb *to be*, *are* is the plural form. (Example: Say, *I am a teacher. She is a student. They are students.*) Invite students to discuss how the verb *to be* is expressed in other languages. Conjugate the verb *to be* in English together.

ACTIVITIES FOR ALL LEARNERS

Favorite Cars
(Kinesthetic/Visual Learners)

Materials: newspapers, magazines, construction paper, scissors, glue

Directions: Divide the class in groups. Ask students to look through the newspapers and magazines for pictures of cars. Have them agree which are their favorites, cut them out, and glue the pictures on a group poster entitled "Our Favorite Cars."

Invite groups to explain their reasons for choosing these cars.

Read It! 🎧

Play the audiocassette of p. 78. Have students (1) read along and listen to the following lines and (2) repeat them as directed. Check pronunciation of the /är/ sound carefully.

> Start the car.   charge card
> farm: barn and garden
> stars in a dark sky
> Arms are part of you.
> 1. The car has a star on the front.
> 2. May's arm is inside the car.
> 3. You start a car with a key.
> 4. The sky is dark when it rains.
> 5. You can shop with a charge card.
> 6. A barn is part of a farm.

Write It!

✏️ Ask students to underline the /är/ words in the sentences on p. 78 and list them on a piece of paper. For homework, you might suggest that they make sentences of their own using each of the words they underlined.

r-Controlled Vowels: /ėr/ er

New Words: summer, winter, weather, mother, sister, her, father, brother

Phonics Objectives

Can students:
- ✓ listen for and identify the /ėr/ sound formed by er?
- ✓ read and write words and sentences with the /ėr/ sound?

Language Acquisition Objectives

Can students:
- ✓ use family words?

Students:
- use the pronoun her
- use words for weather and seasons

ESL Standards
- Goal 2, Standard 2

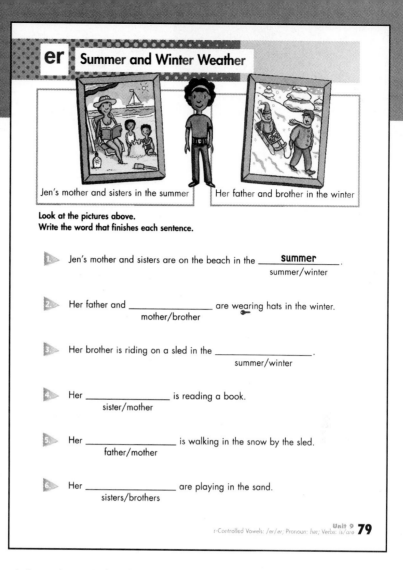

er   Summer and Winter Weather

Jen's mother and sisters in the summer | Her father and brother in the winter

Look at the pictures above.
Write the word that finishes each sentence.

1. Jen's mother and sisters are on the beach in the _____**summer**_____.
   summer/winter

2. Her father and _____ are wearing hats in the winter.
   mother/brother

3. Her brother is riding on a sled in the _____.
   summer/winter

4. Her _____ is reading a book.
   sister/mother

5. Her _____ is walking in the snow by the sled.
   father/mother

6. Her _____ are playing in the sand.
   sisters/brothers

r-Controlled Vowels: /er/ er; Pronoun: her; Verbs: is/are   **Unit 9 79**

BUILDING BACKGROUND

Write the words *summer* and *winter* on the chalkboard. Read the words aloud for the class and ask students to repeat them after you. Point out that the letter combination *er* makes the /ėr/ sound. Explain that *summer* and *winter* are two of the four seasons of the year. What are the other two seasons? Which season is the hottest and which is the coldest? Which months fall in which seasons? Is this the same in all countries?

USING PAGE 79

Ask students to:
- point to the letters *er*
- locate the words as you say them
- read aloud and track words with you

Point out and say the words *mother, sister, father,* and *brother* on p. 79 and stress the /ėr/ sound. Explain that these are all words for family members. Point out that the possessive pronoun *her*

stands for *Jen's.* Remind students that they have learned other possessive pronouns. What are they? (*his, my, your*)

ACTIVITIES FOR ALL LEARNERS

Family Photos
(Kinesthetic/Visual Learners)

Materials: Family photos, light-colored construction paper, pens, tape

Directions: Bring in photos of your family and discuss them with the class. Invite students to bring in their own photos, mount them on construction paper using small rolls of tape (for easy removal), label the pictures, and share them with the class. Students could make diagrams or family trees of their families.

Song: "In the Good Old Summertime" 🎧
(Auditory Learners)

🎵 Play the audiocassette of "In the Good Old Summertime." Distribute copies of the lyrics on p. 101. Be sure stu-

dents understand words like *strolling, shady lanes,* etc. Play the song again and invite students to sing along. Ask them to underline words that contain the /ėr/ sound.

Write It!

✏️ Write the words *brother, sister, father, mother, grandmother,* and *grandfather* on the board. Ask students to copy these sentences and write the name of the family member described in each one.

1. She is married to my father. _____ (*mother*)
2. He is my mother's father. _____ (*grandfather*)
3. My brother and she have the same mother. _____ (*sister*)
4. He is my father's father. _____ (*grandfather*)
5. He is married to my mother. _____ (*father*)
6. My sister and he have the same father. _____ (*brother*)

r-Controlled Vowels: /ėr/ ir, ur

New Words: purple, T-shirt, skirt, purse, girl, sunburn, hurt, nurse, bird

ir | ur   Purple Shirt

a purple T-shirt — skirt — purse — The girl's sunburn hurts. — nurse — bird

Circle *yes* if the sentence is true. Circle *no* if the sentence is not true.

1.	The T-shirt is purple.	(yes)	no
2.	A girl can wear a skirt.	yes	no
3.	A bird can hold a purse.	yes	no
4.	A nurse can drive a car.	yes	no
5.	The girl with the blue shirt is Pat.	yes	no
6.	Her sunburn hurts.	yes	no
7.	The nurse has a purple dress.	yes	no
8.	Pat is wearing a skirt on her arms.	yes	no
9.	A charge card can fit in a purse.	yes	no
10.	A bird can drive a car.	yes	no
11.	Girls can play sports.	yes	no
12.	You can get a sunburn in the summer.	yes	no

80 Unit 9
r-Controlled Vowels: /er/ir, ur: Verbs: *hurt, hold, wear, drive*

FOCUSING ON PHONEMIC AWARENESS

Say the word *shirt* and indicate a student's shirt. Stress the /ėr/ sound. Ask students to listen as you say the following words and raise their hands if they hear the /ėr/ sound as in *shirt, girl, game, skate, skirt, nose, nurse, barn, burn, hand, hurt, peas, purse, bird, bed.*

USING PAGE 80

Ask students to:

• point to the letters *ir* and *ur*
• locate the words as you say them
• read aloud and track words with you

Point out the word *sunburn* on the page and read it aloud. Explain that *sunburn* is a compound word made of two smaller words. Point out that you can tell the meaning of a compound word by exploring the meanings of the smaller words. Ask students to discuss meanings of the smaller words in these words: *classroom,*

baseball, basketball, bedroom. Can students think of other compound words? (*scoreboard, earphones, lunchbox*)

ACTIVITIES FOR ALL LEARNERS

What Am I Wearing Today?
(Auditory/Kinesthetic Learners)

Directions: Divide students into pairs. Explain that they are going to practice clothing and colors by asking, *What am I wearing today?* One partner asks the question and the other responds by pointing and naming each item of clothing with its color. (Example: *You are wearing a white shirt, blue pants, black belt, gold watch . . .*) Have pairs change partners when they finish.

Read It! 🎧

Play the audiocassette of p. 80. Have students (1) read along and listen to the following lines and (2) repeat them as directed. Check pronunciation of the /ėr/ words carefully.

a purple T-shirt skirt purse	
The girl's sunburn hurts. nurse bird	
1. The T-shirt is purple.	yes
2. A girl can wear a skirt.	yes
3. A bird can hold a purse.	no
4. A nurse can drive a car.	yes
5. The girl with the blue shirt is Pat.	yes
6. Her sunburn hurts.	yes
7. The nurse has a purple dress.	no
8. Pat is wearing a skirt on her arms.	no
9. A charge card can fit in a purse.	yes
10. A bird can drive a car.	no
11. Girls can play sports.	yes
12. You can get a sunburn in the summer.	yes

Write It!

Ask students to study the sentences on p. 80 for homework, explaining that you will choose 5 of the sentences for a dictation. Select any 5 sentences and ask students to write them as you dictate them. Have students underline words that have the /ėr/ sound in them. Exchange papers and correct them together as a class.

Review Words: farm, summer, grandpa, grandma/grandmother, are, brother, girl, her, father, mother, over, under, sister, sunburn, weather, bird

New Words: valley, visit, pretty, angel, ripe, wife, change, diaper

Phonics Objectives

Can students:
- ✓ listen for the /är/ and /ėr/ sounds?
- ✓ read words with the letter combinations ar, er, ir, ur in the context of a story?
- ✓ write words with the letter combinations ar, er, ir, ur?

Language Acquisition Objectives

Can students:
- ✓ read words in story context?

ESL Standards

- Goal 1, Standard 2
- Goal 3, Standard 1

Photo Play

A Farm in the Valley

Names in the play: Narrator, Pat, her brother, her brother's wife (and baby), her sister, her mother, her father, her grandfather—Joe, and her grandmother

Narrator: *Pat's father takes the family in the van to visit Grandpa Joe's farm in the valley. It's summer. The valley is hot, but the farm has many old fruit trees. A table is set under the trees.*

Pat:	Hi, Grandpa Joe! Grandma, we are here!
Pat's brother:	And here is my new baby girl!
Brother's wife:	She is just ten weeks old today.
Grandma:	Oh, let me see her. What a pretty baby! She has her father's eyes.
Brother:	And her mother's smile.
Pat's mother:	I am a grandmother, Mama. What do you think of that?
Grandma:	I think that means I am a *great* grandmother. What an angel she is.
Grandpa Joe:	Come over to the table. It's nice under the trees, and we have lots of ripe peaches for you.
Pat's father:	Pat, go help your grandmother with the lunch. Joe and I can watch the baby.
Pat:	Okay, but don't let her get a sunburn. Keep her hat on.
Brother's wife:	And here is a dry diaper if she gets wet.
Pat's sister:	Can Grandpa Joe change a baby?
Grandma:	Sure. Joe likes babies as much as fishing.
Pat's father:	Is this a good year for the fruit, Joe?
Grandpa Joe:	Not bad. We had lots of rain in April and May. Wet weather helps the trees.
Pat's father:	Oh, oh. We have a wet baby. Time to go inside.

Unit 9
r-Controlled Vowels: ar, er, ir, ur **81**

FOCUSING ON PHONEMIC AWARENESS

Song: "Red River Valley" 🎧
(Auditory Learners)

🎵 Play the audiocassette of "Red River Valley." Distribute copies of the lyrics on p. 101. Be sure students understand words like *pathway, awhile, adieu*.

USING THE AUDIOCASSETTE 🎧

Play the song again and invite students to sing along. Ask them to underline words that contain the /ėr/ sound. Explain that this is a cowboy song and that the Red River Valley mentioned in the song is in Texas.

USING THE PHOTO PLAY

🎧 **Preview** the photo play, "A Farm in the Valley," with your students. Allow students time to look through it and examine the picture and text. Ask students to follow along as you play the audiocassette. They may wish to track the words as the play is read.

Background discussion: Ask students if they have ever been on a farm. Where? Was it in a valley? Were there animals on the farm? Do they have family members who live on a farm? Encourage discussion of rural traditions in different countries.

Read the photo play together. Assign volunteers to read the parts of Pat, her brother, her brother's wife, her mother, Grandma, Grandpa Joe, her father, her sister, and the narrator. As students read, listen for correct pronunciation of the /är/ and /ėr/ sounds. Do not interrupt the story, but discuss problem words and errors in pronunciation after the reading. Model the correct pronunciations for students and ask them to repeat the words after you.

Review the story. Lead the class in a second reading of "A Farm in the Valley." This time, ask new volunteers to read the parts.

After they finish reading, ask questions focusing on the content of the story:

- Where is Pat's family going in the van? (*to Grandpa Joe's farm in the valley*)
- What do Pat's brother and his wife have with them? (*A new baby girl*)
- How old is the baby? (*ten weeks*)
- Whose smile does the baby's smile resemble? (*her mother's*)
- Where does Grandpa Joe want to sit? (*at the table under the trees*)
- What does Pat's father offer to do? (*watch the baby*)
- What does Pat's brother's wife give to her father? (*a dry diaper*)
- What does Grandpa Joe say helped the fruit trees? (*wet weather*)
- Why does Pat's father say, "Oh, oh"? (*He has a wet baby.*)

Challenge students to look back through the story and copy down all the words that have the /är/ or /ėr/ sounds in them. When they are finished, review the activity as a class.

r-Controlled Vowels: /är/, /ėr/, ir, ur

Review Words: father, valley, brother, grandmother, Grandma, farm

Phonics Objectives

Can students:
✓ listen for the r-controlled vowels: /är/, /ėr/, ir, ur?
✓ identify the sounds the letters /är/, /ėr/, ir, ur stand for?
✓ read words with the letters /är/, /ėr/, ir, ur in sentences?

Language Acquisition Objectives

Can students:
✓ read and comprehend words in a new context?
✓ write a complete sentence to answer a question?

ESL Standards

• Goal 1, Standard 2

Questions

Finish the sentences using words from the play.

1. Pat's father takes the family to visit _____ .

2. The valley is hot, but _____ .

3. Pat's brother and his wife have a _____ .

4. Pat's grandmother says, "Oh, what a pretty baby! She has _____ ."

5. Pat says to her father, "Don't let her _____ ."

6. Grandma says, "Joe likes _____ ."

To discuss:
• Do you have a big family?
• Does anyone in your family live on a farm?
• Can a man help a lot with a baby?

82 Unit 9
r-Controlled Vowels: ar, er, ir, ur

BUILDING BACKGROUND

Ask students what is happening in the picture at the top of p. 82. Ask if anyone can retell the story on the previous page without turning back to look. Review the events of the photo play together. Ask students if anyone in their family has a new baby. Do they take trips with their family?

USING PAGE 82

Read the instructions to the students. Remind students to make a complete sentence as they answer the questions. They can turn back and reread the story if they need to check an answer. Encourage students to skim the text, looking for key words. Exchange books and go over answers together, as a class. You may wish to use the discussion questions at the bottom of p. 82 for language enrichment. Invite students to explain their answers in detail.

Write a Journal

Invite students to brainstorm stories of family gatherings. Suggest that they write about their experiences in one or two paragraphs in their journals. What was the setting? What sensory memories do they have? (sounds? smells? sights? tastes?) What did family members do and say?

ACTIVITIES FOR ALL LEARNERS

Weather Page: Temperature Graph
(Auditory /Visual Learners)

Materials: daily newspapers, graph paper, pens

Directions: Explain to students that they are going to graph the temperature each day for the next two weeks, using the weather page of the daily newspaper. Show them a model graph with the dates along one axis and the temperature, in increments of 10° Fahrenheit, along the other. Have students make a similar graph.

What is today's temperature? Ask them to locate the point for that temperature on the temperature axis and plot it along the line for today's date. Set aside 5 minutes each day to continue this activity.

CONTENT LINKS

GEOGRAPHY, GEOLOGY

/är/ ar, /ėr/, er
Gateway to Achievement in the Content Areas by Carolyn Bernache: National Textbook Co., 1994
　Parts of the Earth

/ėr/ er, /ėr/ ir, /ėr/ ur
Earth and Physical Science by Mary Ann Christison and Sharon Bassano: Addison Wesley Publishing Co., 1992
　Rivers, Weather and Climate, Water Cycle, The Earth's Surface

Review

r-Controlled Vowels: *ar, er, ir, ur*

New Words: over, under
Review Words: before, after, water

Phonics Objectives

Can students:
- ✓ listen for the /är/ and /èr/ sounds?
- ✓ identify the /är/ and /èr/ sounds formed by different letter combinations?
- ✓ read and write words with *ar, er, ir,* and *ur*?

Language Acquisition Objectives

Can students:
- ✓ use the prepositions *over/under, before/after*?

ESL Standards

- Goal 2, Standard 2

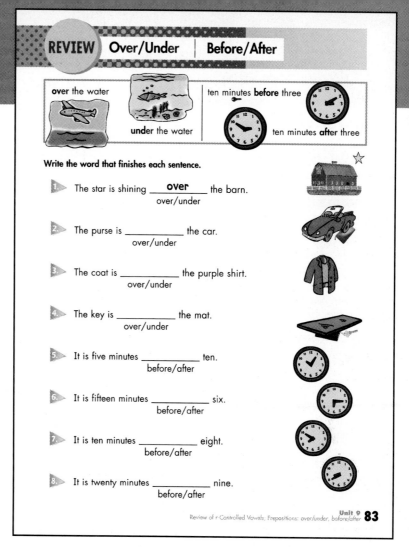

REVIEW | Over/Under | Before/After

over the water
under the water
ten minutes **before** three
ten minutes **after** three

Write the word that finishes each sentence.

1. The star is shining ____**over**____ the barn.
over/under

2. The purse is _____ the car.
over/under

3. The coat is _____ the purple shirt.
over/under

4. The key is _____ the mat.
over/under

5. It is five minutes _____ ten.
before/after

6. It is fifteen minutes _____ six.
before/after

7. It is ten minutes _____ eight.
before/after

8. It is twenty minutes _____ nine.
before/after

Review of r-Controlled Vowels; Prepositions: over/under, before/after **Unit 9 83**

BUILDING BACKGROUND

Place a book on the desk. Put a pen under the book. Say, *The pen is under the book.* Then say, *The book is over the pen.* Move the pen over the book and say, *Now the pen is over the book. What is another word for over?* (*above*) Then say, *The book is under the pen. What is another word for under?* (*below*) Ask a student to place the pen over or under various objects in the class and invite a volunteer to say where it is.

USING THE REVIEW PAGE

Ask students to:
- point to the letters *er*
- locate the words as you say them
- read aloud and track words with you

Ask the class to look at the title of p. 83. Read *over/under* aloud and invite students to repeat it. Use the pictures of the plane over the water and the fish under the water in the box to review the prepositions *over* and *under*. Then read *before/*

after aloud and ask students to repeat it. Explain the prepositions *before* and *after* using the pictures of the clock in the box. Use a teaching clock to show time before and after the hour. Ask students to say the time as you change the clock.

ACTIVITIES FOR ALL LEARNERS

Over or Under?
(Auditory Learners)

Directions: Divide students into pairs. Explain that one partner is going to guess the number—between 1 and 100—that the other has chosen secretly. After each guess, the partner asks if the guess is *over* the amount or *under* it. (Example: Student chooses 28; partner guesses 50; student says *over*, since 50 is over (more than) 28, and so on.) Partners have 10 tries to guess the number.

Read It!

Play the audiocassette of p. 83. Have students (1) read along and listen to the following lines and (2) repeat

them as directed. Check pronunciation of the /èr/ words carefully.

over the water   under the water
ten minutes before three
ten minutes after three

1. The star is shining over the barn.
2. The purse is under the car.
3. The coat is over the purple shirt.
4. The key is under the mat.
5. It is five minutes after ten.
6. It is fifteen minutes after six.
7. It is ten minutes before eight.
8. It is twenty minutes before nine.

Write It!

Write the following sentences on the board. Ask students to use *over, under, before, after* to complete the sentences.

1. When it rains, stay _____ an umbrella. (*under*)
2. The bird flew _____ the tree. (*over*)

Have students write 10 fill-in sentences of their own using *over, under, before, after.*

UNIT 10

Diphthongs: oo, ou, ow, oy, oi

Diphthongs: /ü/ oo

New Words: school, pool, roof, noon, shoot, hoop, food, boots, classroom, cool, tattoo

Phonics Objectives

Can students:
- ✓ listen for the /ü/ sound?
- ✓ identify the /ü/ sound formed by the letter combination oo?
- ✓ read and write words and sentences with the /ü/ sound?

Language Acquisition Objectives

Students:
- use the verb shoot
- use school words school, roof, hoop, classroom, noon, food
- use the clothing word boot

ESL Standards

- Goal 2, Standard 2
- Goal 3, Standard 1

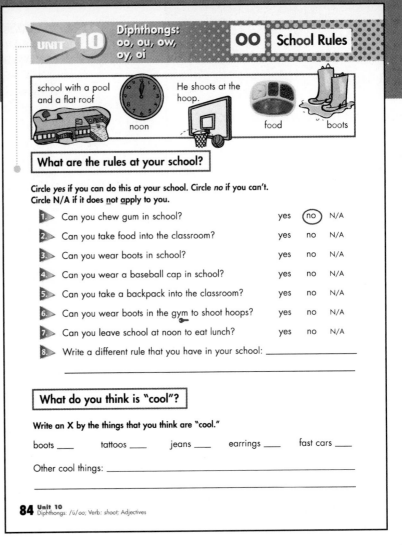

Diphthongs: oo, ou, ow, oy, oi

OO | School Rules

school with a pool and a flat roof

He shoots at the hoop.

noon

food

boots

What are the rules at your school?

Circle *yes* if you can do this at your school. Circle *no* if you can't.
Circle N/A if it does *not* apply to you.

1. Can you chew gum in school? — yes (no) N/A
2. Can you take food into the classroom? — yes no N/A
3. Can you wear boots in school? — yes no N/A
4. Can you wear a baseball cap in school? — yes no N/A
5. Can you take a backpack into the classroom? — yes no N/A
6. Can you wear boots in the gym to shoot hoops? — yes no N/A
7. Can you leave school at noon to eat lunch? — yes no N/A
8. Write a different rule that you have in your school: _____

What do you think is "cool"?

Write an X by the things that you think are "cool."

boots ____   tattoos ____   jeans ____   earrings ____   fast cars ____

Other cool things: _____

84 Unit 10
Diphthongs: /ü/oo; Verb: *shoot*; Adjectives

FOCUSING ON PHONEMIC AWARENESS

Explain that the /ü/ sound in *food* is similar to the long-*u* sound in *flute*. Ask students to repeat the following words after you: *food, pool, school, roof, shoot, hoop, boots*. Ask students to listen to the following words and raise their hand if they hear the /ü/ sound as in *food*: *hop, hoop, beat, boot, sheep, shoot, fit, skin, school, roof, road, plate, pool.*

USING PAGE 84

Ask students to:
- point to the letters *oo*
- locate the words as you say them
- read aloud and track words with you

Ask students to look at the title of the page, "School Rules." Read the title aloud. What are *rules*? What are some school rules? Ask students to give examples of rules they are expected to observe in school. Where else might they find rules?

(*driving—traffic rules, trains—safety rules*) Read the words and phrases in the box at the top of p. 84 aloud, stressing the /ü/ sounds. Have the students repeat the words after you.

ACTIVITIES FOR ALL LEARNERS

Favorite Foods
(Kinesthetic/Visual Learners)

Materials: index cards, paper plates, paper napkins, plastic cups, utensils

Directions: Discuss favorite foods from different countries and suggest that students bring in samples to share. Ask students to write their recipes on the chalkboard and distribute index cards so that others can copy recipes of their favorite foods.

Read It!

Play the audiocassette of p. 84. Have students (1) read along and listen to the following lines and (2) repeat

them as directed. Check pronunciation of the /ü/ sound carefully.

school with a pool and a flat roof   noon
He shoots at the hoop.   food   boots

What are the rules at your school?
1. Can you chew gum in school?
2. Can you take food into the classroom?
3. Can you wear boots in school?
4. Can you wear a baseball cap in school?
5. Can you take a backpack into the classroom?
6. Can you wear boots in the gym to shoot hoops?
7. Can you leave school at noon to eat lunch?
8. Write a different rule that you have in your school.

What do you think is "cool"?
boots tattoos jeans earrings
fast cars

Write It!

Ask students to find the *oo*-words on p. 84, underline them, and write a new sentence of their own for each word.

Diphthongs: /ou/ *ou*

New Words: house, cloud, loud, sound, couch, around, mouse, outside, south, bouncing, ground, bedroom, bathroom, living room, dining room, kitchen

Phonics Objectives

Can students:
- ✓ listen for the /ou/ sound?
- ✓ identify the /ou/ sound formed by the letter combination *ou*?
- ✓ read and write words and sentences with the /ou/ sound?

Language Acquisition Objectives

Can students:
- ✓ use the verb *bounce*?
- ✓ use the preposition *around*?
- ✓ use words referring to a house?
- ✓ use word referring to directions: *south*?

ESL Standards

- Goal 2, Standard 1

ou The House

Write the word that finishes each sentence.

1. The _____couch_____ is in the living room.
   couch/bed

2. The street sign outside the house says _____ Main St.
   West/South

3. The mouse is running _____ the house.
   in/around

4. The bathtub is _____ the house.
   outside/inside

5. The TV has _____ sounds coming from it.
   soft/loud

6. The table is in the _____ of the house.
   dining room/kitchen

7. The dishes are in the _____ in the kitchen.
   sink/bathtub

8. The cloud is _____ the roof of the house.
   above/below

Diphthongs: /ou/ou; Verb: bounce; Preposition: around **Unit 10 85**

FOCUSING ON PHONEMIC AWARENESS

Explain that the letters *ou* together often stand for the /ou/ sound they hear in the word *house*.

Ask students to listen very carefully as you say the following words and raise their hand if they hear the /ou/ sound as in *house*: *mouse, mice, boat, bounce, sand, sound, inside, outside, couch, catch, grain, ground, cloud, clock, around, arm, north, south*.

USING PAGE 85

Ask students to:
- point to the letters *ou*
- locate the words as you say them
- read aloud and track words with you

Ask students to look at the diagram of the house at the top of p. 85. What rooms are shown in the house? (*bedroom, bathroom, living room, dining room, kitchen*)

What *ou*-words are labeled in the illustration? (*house, cloud, loud, sound, outside, south, around, bouncing, couch, mouse, ground*) Can students name other objects in the house that are not labeled? (*bed, TV, bathtub*, etc.) Invite students to discuss houses in their own countries.

ACTIVITIES FOR ALL LEARNERS

Explore Sounds
(Auditory Learners)

Ask the class to sit quietly for a few minutes and listen to the sounds inside and outside the classroom. Were the sounds loud or soft? Were they close or far away? Engage the class in a discussion of the sounds they heard and list them on the board. Ask students what sounds they usually hear at home.

Say It! 🎧

Teach the class the following chant. You may wish to photocopy the words from p. 102 for students.

Group 1: Come on! Come on! Get out of the house!

Group 2: Get out of the house? Why?

Group 1: It's nice outside. Get out of the house!

Group 2: Get out of the house? Why?

Group 1: Don't sit on the couch! Get out of the house!

Group 2: But I like the couch. I like the house.

Group 1: Okay, stay in the house. *I'm going OUT!*

Repeat the chant and ask the groups to exchange parts.

Write It!
Make a Floor Plan

Distribute blank paper and ask students to draw a diagram or floor plan of their own house or apartment. Suggest that they label the rooms, furniture, and outside areas. You might show students a finished diagram or blueprint as a model. Have students share their drawings and discuss them.

Diphthongs: /ou/ *ow*

New Words: how, now, brown, cow, town, down, clown, crown

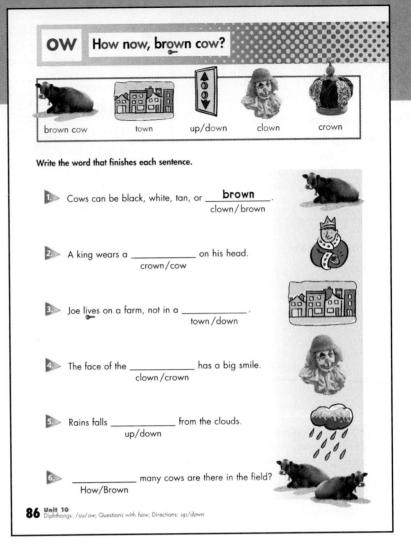

OW How now, brown cow?

brown cow   town   up/down   clown   crown

Write the word that finishes each sentence.

1. Cows can be black, white, tan, or ___**brown**___.
   clown / brown

2. A king wears a _____ on his head.
   crown / cow

3. Joe lives on a farm, not in a _____.
   town / down

4. The face of the _____ has a big smile.
   clown / crown

5. Rains falls _____ from the clouds.
   up / down

6. _____ many cows are there in the field?
   How / Brown

86 Unit 10
Diphthongs: /ou/ ow; Questions with *how*; Directions: *up/down*

FOCUSING ON PHONEMIC AWARENESS

Say the word *down*, stressing the /ou/ sound, and sit down. Point out that the letters *ow* sometimes stand for the /ou/ sound as in *down*. Stand up and ask students, *What am I doing now?* Then sit down again and ask, *And what am I doing now?*

Ask students to listen as you say the following words and raise their hand if the words have the same /ou/ sound as in *down*: cat, *cow*, *now*, new, clear, *clown*, bone, *brown*, cry, *crown*, hot, *how*, *town*, tune.

USING PAGE 86

Ask students to:
- point to the letters *ow*
- locate the words as you say them
- read aloud and track words with you

Read the title of the page, "How now, brown cow?" Explain that *how* is a ques-

tion word like *who, what, when,* or *where.* It expresses degree or manner. The title, a playful use of English sounds, means *How (are you doing), brown cow?* Ask students, *How are you?* What are the usual responses to this question? How is this greeting expressed in other languages? Can students think of another question beginning with *how*? (*How many . . . ? How often . . . ? How do you . . . ?*)

ACTIVITIES FOR ALL LEARNERS

"Ow" Tongue Twisters
(Auditory Learners)

Materials: paper, pens

Directions: Divide the class into pairs. Ask students to read the question, *How now, brown cow?* with you. Repeat it fast and ask students to try to do the same. Explain that this phrase is a "tongue twister," a sentence that is tricky to say because it twists your tongue. Ask each pair to write five tongue twisters of their

own using *ow*-words or *ou*-words. (Example: *The round crown fell down.*) Have groups share their tongue twisters when they finish.

Say It! 🎧

Teach the class the following chant. You may wish to photocopy the words from p. 102 for students.

Group 1: I'm going downtown.
Group 2: Are you leaving now?
Group 1: Yes, I'm walking down.
Group 2: But you're new in town. Do you know how?
Group 1: To get downtown? SURE!

Repeat the chant and ask the groups to exchange parts.

Write It!
Going Downtown

Discuss the lyrics of the chant above. Ask, *Why do you go downtown? For a movie? To go dancing? To shop?* Ask students to write a paragraph about going downtown. Encourage them to include sights, sounds, and feelings.

Diphthongs: /oi/ oy, oi

New Words: joyful, noise, boy, voice, toy, coin, boil

oy | oi Joyful Noises

joyful party noise   a boy's voice   toy drum   coins   boiling water for tea

Write the word that finishes each sentence.

1. Singing is the joyful noise a ___**voice**___ makes.
   voice/coin

2. "Boom" is the loud noise a _____ drum makes.
   toy/joy

3. "Clink" is the noise that _____ make as they drop into a toy bank.
   boys/coins

4. "Yea!" is the noise that _____ and girls yell at a basketball game.
   toys/boys

5. Whistling is the noise a teapot makes when it _____.
   boils/coins

What music makes you joyful?

Write an X by the kinds of music that you like.

rap ____   reggae ____   rock ____   blues ____   jazz ____   gospel ____

classical ____   folk ____   salsa ____   country ____   heavy metal ____

Other kinds of music: _____

_____

Diphthongs: /oi/ oy, oi; Verb: boils **87**
Unit 10

FOCUSING ON PHONEMIC AWARENESS

Explain that *noise* is another word for sound. Pronounce the title, "Joyful Noises," stressing the /oi/ sound in *joyful* and *noise*. Use these words to model oral blending. Ask students to listen carefully to the following words and raise their hand if they hear the /oi/ sound, as in *noise*: *boy, bat, tie, toy, van, voice, coin, cake, boot, boil, jog, joy*.

USING PAGE 87

Ask students to:
- point to the letters *oy* and *oi*
- locate the words as you say them
- read aloud and track words with you

Reread the title, "Joyful Noises." Explain that noises, or sounds, can be happy (joyful) or sad, loud or soft. Can students give examples of joyful noises? (*laughter, music*) Read the words and phrases at the top of p. 87 aloud, stressing the /oi/

sound. Have students reread the words with you; discuss the meanings.

ACTIVITIES FOR ALL LEARNERS

Holiday Toys for Girls and Boys
(Kinesthetic Learners)

Materials: toys to donate

Directions: Suggest that students consider donating toys to needy children at holiday time. Encourage them to discuss the project. (1) How would they organize the donation? (2) What kind of toys should they collect? (3) Which charity should they choose? (4) How should they distribute the toys once they are collected?

Read it! 🎧

Play the audiocassette of p. 87. Have students (1) read along and listen to the following lines and (2) repeat them as directed. Check pronunciation of the /oi/ sound carefully.

joyful party noise   a boy's voice
    toy drum

coins   boiling water for tea
1. Singing is the joyful noise a voice makes.
2. "Boom" is the loud noise a toy drum makes.
3. "Clink" is the noise that coins make as they drop into a toy bank.
4. "Yea!" is the noise that boys and girls yell at a basketball game.
5. Whistling is the noise a teapot makes when it boils.

What music makes you joyful?
   rap   reggae   rock   blues   jazz   gospel   classical   folk   salsa   country   heavy metal

Write It!
Transcribe a Song

✏️ Suggest students bring in CDs or tapes of their favorite songs. After listening to several, have the class choose one to transcribe. (Slower songs are the easiest.) Ask students to listen to each line and tell you what the words are. Write them on the board and have them copy the lines.

Photo Play: "Going Out"

Review Words: out, school, hoop, cool, downtown, house, town, loud, boots, food, pool, room, outside,

New Words: afternoon, store, sale, party, else, guys

Phonics Objectives

Can students:
✓ listen for the /ü/, /ou/, and /oi/ sounds?
✓ read words with the letter combinations oo, ou, ow, oi, and oy in the context of a story?
✓ write words with the letter combinations oo, ou, ow, oi, and oy?

Language Acquisition Objectives

Can students:
✓ read words in story context?
✓ use vocabulary relating to social activities

ESL Standards

• Goal 1, Standard 2

Going Out

Names in the play: Narrator, Pat, Jen, Tom, Will, May, Mike, Steve, Luz

Narrator: *Jen and Pat are walking out of the high school in the afternoon. Tom, Will, May, Mike, Steve, and Luz are waiting for them near the street.*

Jen: I like your new hoop earrings, Pat. They're cool.

Pat: Thanks. I got them on sale at that new store downtown.

Jen: Hey, there's Will. Are you still going out with him?

Pat: Yes, we're going to the party at Tom's house Friday night. Are you coming?

Jen: I think so. Who else is going?

Pat: The rest of the team and a few guys from out of town.

Will: Jen! Pat! Check this out!

Jen: What do you have?

Tom: I have a new CD for the party.

Pat: [*to Jen*] I know it's going to be a loud rock group. All he likes is hard rock.

Luz: Pat, you will love this. It's salsa!

Pat: Cool! Finally Tom has some music I like.

May: What are you wearing Friday, Luz?

Luz: My new boots.

May: But how can you dance in boots?

Luz: Who is going to dance? I'm just going for the food and the pool.

Mike: Tom has a pool?

Steve: Yes. He lives in a town house with a big pool.

Mike: Do they have a game room, too?

Steve: Sure. And a few basketball hoops outside.

Will: Cool! This is going to be a great party.

88 Unit 10
Diphthongs: oo, ou, ow, oy, oi

FOCUSING ON PHONEMIC AWARENESS

Song: "Party Tonight" 🎧
(Auditory Learners)

🎵 Play the audiocassette of the following song.

It's Friday night
Hey, Team, we're going to a party tonight.
The boys are going to make some noise at the party tonight.
The girls are going to rock the house at the party.
Get down and play the music loud at the party tonight.
If the weather's hot, you can come to the pool.
Come on over after school.
Party tonight.

USING THE AUDIOCASSETTE 🎧

Distribute copies of the lyrics on p. 102. Play the song again and invite students to sing along. Ask them to underline words with /ü/, /ou/, and /oi/ sounds.

USING THE PHOTO PLAY

🎧 **Preview** the photo play, "Going Out," with your students. Allow students time to look through it. Ask students to follow along as you play the audiocassette. They may wish to track the words as the play is read.

Background discussion: Ask students if they ever go to parties. Where? When? Do they go with friends or family? What food do they have? What dance music do they like? Encourage discussion of celebrations and parties in different cultures.

Read the photo play together. Assign volunteers to read the parts of Jen, Pat, Will, Tom, Luz, May, Mike, Steve, and the narrator. As students read, listen for correct pronunciation of the /ü/, /ou/, and /oi/ sounds. Do not interrupt the story, but discuss problem words and errors in pronunciation after the reading. Model the correct pronunciations for students and ask them to repeat the words after you.

Review the play. Lead the class in a second reading of "Going Out." This time, ask new volunteers to read the parts. After they finish reading, ask questions focusing on the content of the story:

• Where did Pat buy her hoop earrings? (*at a new store downtown*)
• Where are Pat and Will going Friday night? (*to a party at Tom's house*)
• What kind of music does Tom like? (*hard rock*)
• Who has new boots for the party? (*Luz*)
• Does Tom have a pool at his townhouse? (*yes*)
• Is Luz going to dance at the party? (*no*)
• Why is she going to the party? (*She's just going for the food and the pool.*)

Challenge students to look back through the story and copy down all the words that have the /ü/, /ou/, and /oi/ sounds in them. When they are finished, review the activity as a class.

Questions

Diphthongs: /ü/, /ou/, and /oi/

Review Words: out, boy, town, house, pool, hoop

Questions

Write a sentence to answer each question.

1. What is Pat wearing that Jen likes? ____ Pat is wearing new hoop earrings.

2. What boy is Pat going out with? _____

3. What does Tom have for the party? _____

4. Where is the party Friday night? _____

5. What kind of music do Pat and Luz like? _____

6. What does Tom's town house have besides a pool? _____

To discuss:
- Do you go to parties?
- Do your friends all like the same music?
- Do you like to dance?

Unit 10 Diphthongs: oo, ou, ow, oy, oi **89**

Phonics Objectives

Can students:
- ✓ listen for the diphthongs /ü/, /ou/, and /oi/?
- ✓ identify the sounds the letters *ü, ou,* and *oi* stand for?
- ✓ read words with the letters *ü, ou,* and *oi* in sentences?

Language Acquisition Objectives

Can students:
- ✓ read and comprehend words in a new context?
- ✓ write a complete sentence to answer a question?

ESL Standards

- Goal 1, Standard 2

BUILDING BACKGROUND

Ask students, *Who are the characters in the picture at the top of p. 89?* (*Luz, May, Mike, Tom, Will, Jen, and Pat*) Ask if anyone can retell the story on the previous page without turning back to look. Review the events of the photo play together. Ask students what they do on Friday nights. Do they ever go to parties?

USING PAGE 89

Ask a volunteer to read the instructions and the sample question. Remind students to write a complete sentence as they answer each question. They can reread the story if they need to check an answer. Encourage students to skim the text, looking for key words. Exchange books and go over answers together, as a class. You may wish to use the discussion questions at the bottom of p. 89 for language enrichment.

Read It! 🎧

🙂 Play the audiocassette of p. 89. Have students (1) read along and listen to the following lines and (2) repeat them as directed. Check pronunciation of the /ü/, /ou/, and /oi/ sounds carefully.

1. What is Pat wearing that Jen likes?
2. What boy is Pat going out with?
3. What does Tom have for the party?
4. Where is the party Friday night?
5. What kind of music do Pat and Luz like?
6. What does Tom's town house have besides a pool?

Write It!
A Journal

✏️ Invite students to brainstorm stories of social gatherings—parties, proms, weddings, and other celebrations. Suggest that they write about their experiences in their journals. What was the setting? What sensory memories do they have of the party? (sounds? smells? sights? tastes?)

CONTENT LINKS

FOOD and RECIPES
/ü/ /ou /

Simple French Food by Richard Olney et al.: Hungry Minds Inc., 1992

Knife, Fork, and Spoon: Eating Around the World by Charles Baker: Derrydale Press, 2001

Around the World Cookbook by the Lorenz Books Staff: Lorenz Books, 2000

Cooking Without Borders by the Atlanta International School, 1999

Lonely Planet World Food: Mexico by Bruce Geddas and Paloma Garcia: Lonely Planet, 2000

/oi/

The Joy of Cooking by Irma S. Rombauer and Marion Rombauer Becker: Plume, 1997

Review

Diphthongs: *oo, ou, ow, oy, oi*

Review Words: cow, school, pool, brown, couch, cloud, hoop, noon, food, boots, mouse, voice, bounce, noise, toy, coin

BUILDING BACKGROUND

Ask the class if they remember what a riddle is. Refer to the examples which students did in Unit 6, p. 52. Ask them if they know another riddle. Explain that the box at the top of this Review page contains the answers to the riddles below it.

USING THE REVIEW PAGE

Ask students to:
- • point to the letters *oo, ou, ow, oy, oi*
- • locate the words in the box at the top of the page as you say them
- • read aloud and track words with you

Read the instructions. Ask a volunteer to read sentence 1—the sample riddle and its answer. Ask students to read sentence 2

cow	school	pool	brown	couch	cloud
hoop	noon	~~food~~	boots	mouse	
voice	bounce	noise	toy	coin	

Write the word from the box that answers the question.

1. It can be meat or fruit on a plate that you eat for lunch. It is __food__.

2. You can swim in it, and it has water in it. It is a _____.

3. It means the same as twelve o'clock midday. It is _____.

4. It is a little animal that likes to eat cheese. It is a _____.

5. You wear them on your feet in the rain. They are _____.

6. It is like a long chair that you sit on to watch TV. It is a _____.

7. It is the place you go to study and take classes. It is _____.

8. You can use it to pay for a bus ride. It is a _____.

9. It is a big, black, brown, or tan animal that gives milk. It is a _____.

10. A baby or little child likes to play with it. It is a _____.

11. It is a lot of loud sounds that you hear in a town. It is _____.

12. It is a singing or talking sound. It is a _____.

13. It floats high in the sky on a nice day. It is a _____.

14. It is round, with a basketball net on it. It is a _____.

15. It is a color that is used for shoes and floors. It is _____.

16. A ball can do this when it hits the floor. It can _____.

90 Unit 10
Review of Diphthongs

---

aloud with you. Can someone answer the riddle by referring to the words in the box? Ask students to try to answer the rest of the riddles by reading each description on their own. They may consult with a friend if they need help. Correct answers together and discuss the riddles.

Write it!

Ask students to reread the sentences on p. 90 and underline the words that contain the /ü/, /ou/, and /oi/ sounds. Next, have them fold a piece of notepaper vertically into three columns. At the top of each column have them write one of the three diphthongs: /ü/, /ou/, or /oi/. Ask them to classify the underlined words from p. 90 by sound and list them under the appropriate heading. (Example, sentence 1: *fruit, you, food,* under the /ü/ sound.) You might remind them that long-*u* and the *oo*-diphthong both have the /ü/ sound.

Answer Key for Student Book

UNIT 1 — Short Vowels: a, o, i

page 2 – 2. a 3. f 4. b 5. d 6. e
page 3 – 2. cat 3. bat 4. van 5. hat 6. map
page 4 – 2. f 3. a 4. c 5. b 6. e
page 5 – 2. can 3. can 4. cannot 5. cannot 6. cannot
page 6 – 2. c 3. e 4. f 5. a 6. d
page 7 – 2. is 3. is 4. is 5. is 6. is
page 8 – 2. b 3. a 4. c; 2. off 3. on
page 10 – 2. no 3. no 4. yes 5. no 6. yes 7. yes 8. no 9. yes
    10. no
page 11 – 2. f 3. a 4. b 5. e 6. c 7. h 8. g

UNIT 2 — Short Vowels: u, e

page 12 – 2. d 3. a 4. e 5. f 6. c
page 13 – 2. rug 3. sun 4. mud 5. bug 6. box
page 14 – 2. d 3. e 4. a 5. f 6. b
page 15 – 2. no 3. no 4. yes 5. no 6. yes
page 16 – 2. bed 3. eggs 4. bags 5. a dog 6. cats 7. nets
    8. bugs
page 18 – 2. not 3. bed 4. Bud 5. leg 6. hill 7. run 8. wet
    9. on 10. sun
page 19 – 2. a 3. h 4. f 5. g 6. c 7. d 8. e

UNIT 3 — Blends

page 20 – 2. f 3. e 4. c 5. d 6. a
page 21 – 2. no 3. yes 4. no 5. yes 6. no 7. no 8. no
    9. yes 10. yes
page 22 – 2. d 3. a 4. e 5. f 6. b
page 23 – 2. d 3. b 4. f 5. a 6. c
page 24 – 2. jump 3. milk 4. gift 5. drinks 6. swim
page 25 – 2. belt 3. tent 4. nest 5. Help 6. desk
page 26 – 2. no 3. yes 4. no 5. no 6. no 7. no 8. no
    9. yes 10. no
page 28 – 1. 7 2. 8 4. 10 5. 2 6. 9 7. 5 8. 3 9. 6 10. 4
page 29 – 2. hit 3. run 4. bus 5. pens 6. grass 7. desk
    8. class 9. sits 10. dress

UNIT 4 — Long Vowels: a

page 30 – 2. d 3. f 4. b 5. a 6. e
page 31 – 2. red 3. tray 4. say 5. wakes 6. cake
page 32 – 2. e 3. b 4. a 5. f 6. c
page 33 – 2. yes 3. no 4. no; 2. pens 3. hats
page 34 – 2. d 3. a 4. c; 2. run 3. snack
page 37 – 2. yes 3. no 4. yes 5. no 6. yes 7. no 8. yes
    9. no 10. no

UNIT 5 — Long Vowels: i

page 38 – 2. a 3. f 4. b 5. d 6. c
page 39 – 2. tires 3. I 4. fly 5. smile 6. cries
page 40 – 2. night 3. light 4. bright 5. high 6. right
page 41 – 2. no 3. yes 4. no 5. yes 6. no 7. no 8. yes
    9. no 10. yes 11. no 12. yes
page 42 – 2. sand 3. wide 4. face 5. man 6. bag 7. sky
    8. tire 9. nine 10. jog 11. hot 12. page
    13. run 14. train 15. night 16. day 17. class
    18. snail
page 44 – 2. wait 3. job 4. black 5. red 6. Nine 7. fly 8. rock
    9. tire 10. help
page 45 – Answers will vary.

UNIT 6 — Long Vowels: o, e, u

page 46 – 2. c 3. f 4. a 5. b 6. e
page 47 – 2. snow 3. blow 4. yellow 5. grow 6. go
page 48 – 2. yes 3. no 4. yes 5. yes 6. no 7. yes
    8. no 9. yes 10. no 11. no 12. yes
page 49 – 2. big 3. no 4. cold 5. cannot 6. is 7. back 8. go
    9. on 10. slow 11. rain 12. hold 13. day 14. sad
    15. ride 16. ice
page 50 – 2. e 3. d 4. c 5. f 6. a
page 51 – 2. yes 3. no 4. yes 5. no 6. no 7. yes 8. yes
    9. yes 10. yes
page 52 – 2. hockey 3. twenty 4. study 5. baby 6. monkey
page 53 – 2. see 3. hear 4. beard 5. years 6. tears
page 54 – 2. a 3. d 4. f 5. b 6. e
page 55 – Answers will vary.
page 56 – 2. happy 3. low 4. sunny 5. above 6. hold
    7. do 8. hot 9. behind 10. day 11. huge
    12. wait 13. sleep 14. ride 15. get on 16. fast
page 59 – 2. field 3. plate 4. go 5. wide 6. wait 7. strikes
    8. floats 9. tree 10. home

UNIT 7   Digraphs: sh, ph, th

page 60 – 2. e 3. b 4. f 5. a 6. c
page 61 – Mike: bat; Steve: mitt; Mike: she; Steve: can't;
              Mike: field; Steve: bike
page 62 – 2. yes 3. no 4. yes 5. no 6. no
page 63 – 2. lake 3. sand 4. flute 5. baby 6. ball 7. shoes
              8. fish
page 64 – 2. splash 3. hat 4. few 5. make 6. top 7. boat
              8. grow 9. math 10. sleep 11. line 12. tree
              13. float 14. nose
page 66 – 2. wash 3. Roth 4. fish 5. Beth 6. throws 7. shakes
              8. bathtub 9. movies 10. phone
page 67 – 2. blue shoes 3. yellow rain hat 4. green shoes
              5. red and blue cap 6. black coat 7. red shoes

UNIT 8   Digraphs: wh, ng, ch, tch, wr, kn

page 68 – 2. h 3. a 4. f 5. c 6. d 7. e 8. g
page 69 – Answers will vary.
page 70 – 2. string 3. song 4. ring 5. hungry 6. long
page 71 – 2. c 3. d 4. e 5. b 6. f 7. j 8. g 9. a 10. i
page 72 – 2. lunchbox 3. peach 4. check 5. chicken 6. cheese
page 73 – 2. watch 3. scratch 4. match 5. crutches 6. watch
page 74 – 2. wrong 3. wrong 4. right 5. wrong 6. wrong
              7. wrong 8. right 9. right 10. right 11. wrong
              12. right 13. wrong 14. right
page 76 – Will can't walk. 3. The pain is his right knee. 4. It feels
              like a knife is in the knee. 5. An X-ray is like a photo of
              the knee. 6. Will's baseball game is on Friday.
page 77 – 2. when 3. that 4. shake 5. king 6. song 7. shine
              8. bath 9. wheat 10. write 11. shoe 12. sheep
              13. knee 14. know 15. dash 16. scratch 17. walking
              18. flying 19. hopping 20. snowing 21. playing
              22. thinking 23. these 24. taking

UNIT 9   r-Controlled Vowels: ar, er, ir, ur

page 78 – 2. a 3. e 4. b 5. f 6. d
page 79 – 2. brother 3. winter 4. mother 5. father 6. sisters
page 80 – 2. yes 3. no 4. yes 5. yes 6. yes 7. no 8. no
              9. yes 10. no 11. yes 12. yes
page 82 – 1. Grandpa Joe's farm in the valley. 2. the farm has
              many old fruit trees. 3. new baby girl 4. her father's
              eyes 5. get a sunburn 6. babies as much as fishing
page 83 – 2. under 3. over 4. under 5. after 6. after 7. before
              8. before

UNIT 10   Dipthongs: oo, ou, ow, oy, oi

page 84 – Answers will vary.
page 85 – 2. South 3. around 4. inside 5. loud 6. dining room
              7. sink 8. above
page 86 – 2. crown 3. town 4. clown 5. down 6. How
page 87 – 2. toy 3. coins 4. boys 5. boils; Answers will vary.
page 89 – 2. Will 3. Tom has a new CD 4. The party is at Tom's
              house. 5. Pat and Luz like salsa music. 6. Tom's
              house has a game room and a few basketball hoops
              outside.
page 90 – 2. pool 3. noon 4. mouse 5. boots 6. couch
              7. school 8. coin 9. cow 10. toy 11. noise
              12. voice 13. cloud 14. hoop 15. brown 16. bounce

Songs and Chants

UNIT 1

This Land Is Your Land

Chorus

This land is your land,
This land is my land,
From California
To the New York Island
From the redwood forest
To the gulfstream waters,
This land was made for you and me.

As I went walking
That ribbon of highway
I saw above me
That endless skyway
I saw below me
That golden valley,
This land was made for you and me.

Chant

[Group 1:] I can hop. Hop, hop, hop!
[Group 2:] I can jog. Jog, jog, jog!
[Group 1:] I can mop. Mop, mop, mop.
[Group 2:] But I'm hot! Hot, hot, hot!

Chant

[Group 1:] Pat has a bat and a map and a pan.
[Group 2:] Pat has a bag and a hat and a mitt.
[Group 1:] Will it all fit in the van?
[Group 2:] Will it all fit in the van?

Chant

[Group 1:] Hey, Jen! … Jen!
              Can you jog?
[Group 2:] Jog? I can't jog.
[Group 1:] Why not?
[Group 2:] I'm in bed.
[Group 1:] Bed?
[Group 2:] I have a bad leg.
[Group 1:] Bad leg?
[Group 2:] Yes.
[Group 1:] You're stuck in bed?
[Group 2:] Yes, and I'm MAD!

UNIT 3

You're a Grand Old Flag

You're a grand old flag, you're a high flying flag
And forever, in peace, may you wave.
You're the emblem of the land I love,
The home of the free and the brave.
Every heart beats true, under red, white, and blue
Where there's never a boast or brag,
But should auld acquaintance be forgot,
Keep your eye on the grand old flag.

Swing Low, Sweet Chariot

Chorus
Swing low, sweet chariot,
Comin' for to carry me home;
Swing low, sweet chariot,
Comin' for to carry me home.

I looked over Jordan and what did I see?
Comin' for to carry me home;
A band of angels comin' after me,
Comin' for to carry me home.

If you get there before I do,
Comin' for to carry me home;
Tell all my friends I'm a-comin' too,
Comin' for to carry me home.

Chant

[Group 1:]   I have a friend
[Group 2:]   Who runs very fast.
[Group 1:]   He's quick! [clap, clap]
[Group 2:]   He's quick! [clap, clap]
[Group 1:]   He's always first.
[Group 2:]   He's never last.
[Group 1:]   He's quick! [clap, clap]
[Group 2:]   He's quick! [clap, clap]

The Pick-up Truck

Poor old Tom is out of luck
He's got a problem with his pick-up truck
He's got a job at seven o'clock
But his truck just runs and stops.

He steps off the truck
Stands next to the back
He looks at the sand and the bricks and the sticks.
He jumps back in and yells at the truck.

It's seven o'clock and Tom is out of luck.
Hey! Can you move that truck?

Chant

[Group 1:] It's such a gray [clap, clap] gray day. [clap, clap]

[Group 2:] We have to stay [clap, clap] inside today. [clap, clap]

[Group 1:] Inside the house [clap, clap] on this gray day. [clap, clap]

[Group 2:] This is no fun [clap, clap], NO WAY! [clap, clap]

Chant

[Group 1:] No need to wait. You have e-mail.

[Group 2:] You've got mail. You've got mail.

[Group 1:] It's never late in rain or hail.

[Group 2:] You've got mail. You've got mail.

[Group 1:] This is great! It cannot fail!

[Group 2:] You've got mail. You've got mail.

Chant

[Group 1:] Is it big?

[Group 2:] No, it's not.

[Group 1:] Let's see. What can it be? Can it run?

[Group 2:] No, it can't.

[Group 1:] Let's see. What can it be? Is it a pan? Is it a pot?

[Group 2:] No, it isn't. No, it's not.

A Day at the Lake

May tells Pat, "Let's have a picnic at the lake."
Pat says, "Great!"
Tom can't take the truck so they take the van.
That's okay.

Snacks and drinks and grapes and cakes and waves in the lake.
Snacks and drinks and grapes and cakes and waves in the lake.
Look at Bud. What's this? Look at Bud.
Has he got a snake?
No, it's a stick! Let's take a break!
No, it's a stick! Let's take a break!

They play all day and then the sky turns gray.
They play all day and then the sky turns gray.
A day at the lake then comes to an end.
A day at the lake then comes to an end.
It looks like rain. Can't wait to do it again!

UNIT 5

Chant

[Group 1:]   Star light, star bright.
[Group 2:]   First star I see tonight.
[Group 1:]   Wish I may. Wish I might.
[Group 2:]   Have the wish I wish tonight.

My Bike

A bright red truck
Drives by my bright red bike
My eyes light up
And I smile a mile wide
I fly my bike
In day or night
I ride so fast
That my tires catch fire!

Row, Row, Row Your Boat

Row, row, row your boat
Gently down the stream.
Merrily, merrily, merrily, merrily,
Life is but a dream.

Chant

[Group 1:] The baseball score was four to four.
[Group 2:] The crowd began to roar.
[Group 1:] Then they scored another four.
[Group 2:] But we came back with more.

Rock-a-bye Baby

Rock-a-bye baby on the tree top,
When the wind blows
The cradle will rock.
When the bough breaks,
The cradle will fall,
And down will come baby,
Cradle and all.

Home on the Range

Oh, give me a home, where the buffalo roam,
Where the deer and the antelope play,
Where seldom is heard a discouraging word,
And the skies are not cloudy all day.

Chorus

Home, home on the range,
Where the deer and the antelope play,
Where seldom is heard a discouraging word,
And the skies are not cloudy all day.

How often at night when the heavens are bright
With the light of the glittering stars,
Have I stood here amazed and asked as I gazed
If their glory exceeds that of ours.

Chant

[Group 1:] Do you like soup?
[Group 2:] Yes I do. I really like soup.
         Do you?
[Group 1:] No, I don't. I really don't.
         But I like juice. Do you?
[Group 2:] Yes, I like juice
         And I like soup.
         I really like soup.
         Why don't you?

Chant

[Group 1:] Something old
[Group 2:] Something new
[Group 1:] Something borrowed
[Group 2:] Something blue
[Group 1:] Silver sixpence in your shoe.

Take Me Out to the Ball Game

Take me out
To the ball game.
Take me out
With the crowd.
Buy me some peanuts
And Crackerjacks;
I don't care if
I never get back.

Let me root, root, root
For the home team;
If they don't win
It's a shame,
For it's one, two,
Three strikes you're out
At the old ball game!

UNIT 7

Chant

[Group 1:]   He's my friend through thick and thin.
[Group 2:]   Thick and thin, thick and thin.
[Group 1:]   He's my friend through thick and thin.
[Group 2:]   He'll always be my friend.

Deep In the Heart of Texas

The stars at night are big and bright,   [clap, clap, clap, clap]
Deep in the heart of Texas,
The prairie sky is wide and high,   [clap, clap, clap, clap]
Deep in the heart of Texas.
The sage in bloom is like perfume,   [clap, clap, clap, clap]
Deep in the heart of Texas,
Reminds me of the one I love,   [clap, clap, clap, clap]
Deep in the heart of Texas.

Splash, Splash

Hey, May, can you baby-sit today?
I'll be there at three o'clock.
Three o'clock?
Splash, splash, give the baby a bath
Let her play in the tub-tub-tub. Yeah!
Wash her ears and wash her nose.
Wash her fingers and wash her toes.
Splash, splash, time to get out of the bath.
I have to get that telephone!

Chant

[Group 1:]   What's this? What's this?
[Group 2:]   It's a shirt. It's a shirt.
[Group 1:]   What's that? What's that?
[Group 2:]   It's a skirt. It's a skirt.
[Group 1:]   What are these? What are these?
[Group 2:]   They're my shoes. They're my shoes.
[Group 1:]   What are those? What are those?
[Group 2:]   Oh, those? Who knows?

Chant

[Group 1:]   What time is it? What time is it?
[Group 2:]   It's seven o'clock. It's time for the bus.
[Group 1:]   What time is it? What time is it?
[Group 2:]   It's eight o'clock. Don't wait for us.

Long, Long Trail

There's a long, long trail a-winding into the land of
my dreams,
Where the nightingales are singing and the white
moon beams,
There's a long, long night a-waiting until my
dreams all come true,
And that's the day when I'll be going down that
long, long trail with you.

Chant

[Group 1:]   A chicken wing, an onion ring,
[Group 2:]   A slice of cheese to munch.
[Group 1:]   A peach or two, a bowl of stew,
[Group 2:]   Now that's a tasty lunch!

Chant

[Group 1:]   She's never wrong.
[Group 2:]   She's always right.
[Group 1:]   She's perfect as can be.
[Group 2:]   She knows it all.
[Group 1:]   She's very bright.
[Group 2:]   Almost as bright as me!

Bad Knee Blues

I went to the doctor
To check out my knee.
"What's wrong?" said the doctor.
The pain is killing me.
The doctor said that I can't play
And now I need to get an X-ray.

When I bend down to catch the ball.
When I stand up and walk down the hall.
The doctor said that I can't play
And now I need to get an X-ray.

UNIT 9

In the Good Old Summertime

In the good old summertime,
In the good old summertime,
Strolling through the shady lanes,
With your baby mine.

You hold her hand and she holds yours,
And that's a very good sign,
That she's your tootsie-wootsie
In the good old summertime.

Red River Valley

From this valley they say you are going.
We will miss your bright eyes and sweet smile
For they say you are taking the sunshine
That has brightened our pathways awhile.

Chorus
Come and sit by my side if you love me.
Do not hasten to bid me adieu.
Just remember the Red River Valley
And the cowboy who loved you so true.

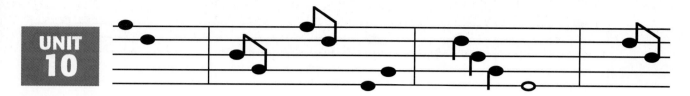

UNIT 10

Chant

[Group 1:] Come on! Come on! Get out of the house!
[Group 2:] Get out of the house? Why?
[Group 1:] It's nice outside. Get out of the house!
[Group 2:] Get out of the house? Why?
[Group 1:] Don't sit on the couch! Get out of the house!
[Group 2:] But I like the couch. I like the house.
[Group 1:] Okay, stay in the house. I'm going OUT!

Chant

[Group 1:] I'm going downtown
[Group 2:] Are you leaving now?
[Group 1:] Yes, I'm walking down.
[Group 2:] But you're new in town.
 Do you know how?
[Group 1:] To get downtown? SURE!

Party Tonight

It's Friday night
Hey, Team, we're going to a party tonight (party, party)
It's Friday night
Hey, Team, we're going to a party tonight.

The boys are going to make some noise at the party tonight
(party, party)
The girls are going to rock the house at the party.
The boys are going to make some noise at the party tonight
(party, party)
The girls are going to rock the house at the party.

Get down and play the music loud at the party tonight
If the weather's hot, you can come to the pool.
Come on over after school.
Party tonight.

Assessment

UNIT 1 Short Vowels: a, o, i

Circle the word that matches the picture.

1. hot   (hat)   hit

2. bat   mat   cat

3. map   man   mat

4. mat   hill   mitt

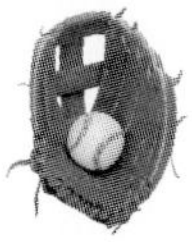

5. dog   mop   pot

6. six   fox   box

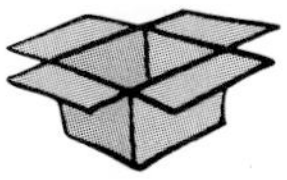

7. man   pan   van

8. Will   hill   ball

9. pot   rock   jog

10. bag   dog   big

| bed | gum | bus | leg | pen | egg | rug | tub | bug | men | sun | ten |

Write the word from the box that matches each picture.

1. _____bed_____

2. _____

3.  _____

4.  _____

5. _____

6. _____

7.  _____

UNIT 3 Blends

Make an X by the sentence that matches each picture.

1. _____ The frog is in the box.

   ___X___ The frog is in the grass.

2. _____ The plant is on the desk.

   _____ The plant is on the dress.

3. _____ Will has a brick.

   _____ Will has a gift.

4. _____ The crab is on the steps.

   _____ The crab is on the sand.

5. _____ Bud is next to the sled.

   _____ Tom is next to the sled.

6. _____ It is ten o'clock.

   _____ It is six o'clock.

7. _____ A stick is on the rock.

   _____ A stick is on the steps.

8. _____ Will can swim.

   _____ Will can jump.

UNIT 4 Long Vowels: a

| wakes | takes | makes | snake | waits | great | plays | ~~say~~ | rain | face |

Write the word from the box that completes each sentence.

1. Bob and Nan _____say_____ , "Hey, May!"

2. May _____ up at 6:00.

3. May _____ a red pen off the desk.

4. May _____ at the bus stop.

5. Bud runs in the _____ and gets wet.

6. May _____ baseball.

7. The sun is up, and it's a _____ day.

8. May has a happy _____ .

9. A big, gray _____ is in the grass.

10. May _____ a cake.

UNIT5   Long Vowels: i

RHYMES

Say each word. Circle the two words that rhyme.
Write the two rhyming words on the line.

1. line   (bike)   lake   (like)   _____ bike _____ like _____

2. cry   ride   ice   sky   _____

3. like   fire   tire   five   _____

4. light nine   wide   night _____

5. hide   smile   high   side   _____

6. face   mice   ice   my   _____

7. nine   line   night smile _____

8. mice   Mike   by   my   _____

9. ride   right   side   five   _____

10. bike   eye   bite   pie   _____

11. five   high   my   fire   _____

12. sign   line   side   sky   _____

13. drive like   ride   five   _____

14. time   bite   sign   bright _____

UNIT6 Long Vowels: o, e, u

ROSE / HOP

~~rope~~	~~dog~~	goat	jog	hot	soap	pot	stove
snow	frog	road	cold	go	nose	rock	box

Say each word in the box above.
If the word has a long-o sound, write it on the line after "rose."
If it has a short-o sound, write it on the line after "hop."

o like R**o**se   _rope_ _____

o like h**o**p   _dog_ _____

GET / GREEN

~~feet~~	~~bed~~	he	leg	men	tree	pen	team
eat	field	red	see	ten	sleep	sled	meat

Say each word in the box above.
If the word has a long-e sound, write it on the line after "green."
If it has a short-e sound, write it on the line after "get."

e like gr**ee**n   _feet_ _____

e like g**e**t   _bed_ _____

UNIT 7 Digraphs: sh, ph, th

Make an *X* by the sentence that matches each picture.

1.

_____ A sheep is by the boat.

_____ A ship is by the boat.

___X___ A shoe is by the boat.

2.

_____ A fish is on the dish.

_____ A fish is on the dress.

_____ A fish is on the desk.

3.

_____ Mike has elephants.

_____ Mike has telephones.

_____ Mike has earphones.

4.

_____ The baby takes a bat.

_____ The baby takes a bath.

_____ The baby takes a bus.

5.

_____ Bud swims with Tom.

_____ Bud splashes with Tom.

_____ Bud races with Tom.

6.

_____ A brush is on the ship.

_____ A brush is on the shelf.

_____ A brush is on the dish.

UNIT 8   Digraphs: wh, ng, ch, tch, wr, kn

Write the word that completes each sentence.

1. A _____ whale _____ is a big sea animal like a fish.
    whale / wheel

2. An umpire blows a _____ to stop a game.
    whistle / wheel

3. A _____ is long, like a rope.
    swing / string

4. Luz is happy when she is _____ a song.
    singing / washing

5. Steve has a _____ sandwich in his lunchbox.
    beach / cheese

6. Tom has a _____ that says three o'clock.
    watch / match

7. You can _____ with a pen.
    right / write

8. You can eat meat with a _____ and fork.
    knee / knife

9. You sign your name on a _____ .
    chicken / check

10. You use _____ to make a fire.
    crutches / matches

MONTHS AND WEATHER

January	April	July	October
February	May	August	November
March	June	September	December

Say the months with your teacher. Then read the phrases below.

birds making nests	snow on the trees	gardens with big corn
ice on the car windows	new baby farm animals	yellow leaves blowing
hot days at the beach	sunburn on your arms	dark sky and clear stars

Write the phrases that match the months where you live.

1. March, April, May _birds making nests_ _____

   _____

2. December, January, February _____

   _____

3. June, July, August _____

   _____

4. September, October, November _____

   _____

UNIT 10 Diphthongs: oo, ou, ow, oy, oi

Write the word that completes each sentence.

1. I put on my brown _____*boots*_____ to go out in the rain.
   boots / boats

2. My lunchbox has _____ and a drink in it.
   roof / food

3. The team _____ when the ball goes in the hoop.
   shouts / crown

4. Luz hears the loud _____ of thunder outside.
   town / sound

5. The clock has numbers all _____ it.
   around / under

6. Pat's bag is _____ on the floor by her desk.
   clown / down

7. The voices in the class make _____.
   noise / rose

8. The sign on the door of the toilet says "_____" on it.
   Cows / Boys

9. Will likes to swim in a _____.
   pool / pail

10. She _____ a basketball at the hoop.
    shouts / shoots

Assessment Answer Key

UNIT 1   Short Vowels: a, o, i

page 103 – 2. cat 3. man 4. mitt 5. mop 6. box 7. van 8. ball 9. rock 10. bag

UNIT 2   Short Vowels: u, e

page 104 – 2. sun 3. bus 4. tub 5. pen 6. leg 7. rug

UNIT 3   Blends

page 105 – 2. The plant is on the desk. 3. Will has a gift. 4. The crab is on the sand.
5. Tom is next to the sled. 6. It is ten o'clock. 7. A stick is on the steps. 8. Will can swim.

UNIT 4   Long Vowels: a

page 106 – 2. wakes 3. takes 4. waits 5. rain 6. plays 7. great 8. face 9. snake 10. makes

UNIT 5   Long Vowels: i

page 107 – 2. cry/sky 3. fire/tire 4. light/night 5. hide/side 6. mice/ice 7. nine/line 8. by/my
9. ride/side 10. eye/pie 11. high/my 12. sign/line 13. drive/five 14. bite/bright

UNIT 6   Long Vowels: o, e, u

page 108 – o like rose: goat, soap, stove, snow, cold, road, go, nose
o like hop: jog, hot, pot, frog, rock, box
e like green: he, tree, team, eat, field, see, sleep, meat
e like get: leg, men, pen, red, ten, sled

UNIT 7   Digraphs: sh, ph, th

page 109 – 2. A fish is on the dish. 3. Mike has earphones. 4. The baby takes a bath. 5. Bud races with Tom.
6. A brush is on the shelf.

UNIT 8   Digraphs: wh, ng, ch, tch, wr, kn

page 110 – 2. whistle 3. string 4. singing 5. cheese 6. watch 7. write 8. knife 9. check 10. matches

UNIT 9   r-Controlled Vowels: ar, er, ir, ur

page 111 – Answers will vary.

UNIT 10   Diphthongs: oo, ou, ow, oy, oi

page 112 – 2. food 3. shouts 4. sound 5. around 6. down 7. noise 8. Boys 9. pool 10. shoots

ESL Standards

National TESOL ESL Goals and Standards for Pre-K–12 Students

The following is excerpted with permission from *ESL Standards for Pre-K–12 Students* published by Teachers of English to Speakers of Other Languages, Inc. copyright 1997.

(TESOL refers to teachers of English to speakers of other languages. ESL refers to English as a second language. ESOL refers to English to speakers of other languages.)

Goals for ESOL Learners

TESOL has established three broad goals for ESOL learners at all age levels—goals that include personal, social, and academic uses of English. Each goal is associated with three distinct standards. In TESOL's vision, ESOL learners will meet these standards as a result of the instruction they receive, thereby achieving the goals. Our schools need to ensure that all students achieve the English language competence needed for academic success and for life in a literate culture.

Goal 1:
To use English to communicate in social settings

A primary goal of ESL instruction is to assist students in communicating effectively in English, both in and out of school. Such communication is vital if ESOL learners are to avoid the negative social and economic consequences of low proficiency in English and are to participate as informed participants in our democracy. ESOL learners also need to see that there are personal rewards to be gained from communicating effectively in English. This goal does not suggest, however, that students should lose their native language proficiency.

Standards for Goal 1

Students will:

1. use English to participate in social interaction

2. interact in, through, and with spoken and written English for personal expression and enjoyment

3. use learning strategies to extend their communicative competence

Goal 2:
To use English to achieve academically in all content areas

In school settings, English competence is critical for success and expectations for ESOL learners are high. They are expected to learn academic content through the English language and to compete academically with native-English-speaking peers. This process requires that learners use spoken and written English in their schoolwork.

Standards for Goal 2

Students will:

1. use English to interact in the classroom

2. use English to obtain, process, construct, and provide subject matter information in spoken and written form

3. use appropriate learning strategies to construct and apply academic knowledge

Goal 3:
To use English in socially and culturally appropriate ways

ESOL students in U.S. schools come into contact with peers and adults who are different from them, linguistically and culturally. The diversity in U.S. schools mirrors the diversity in this country and around the world that young people will encounter as they move into the twenty-first century world of work. In order to work and live amid diversity, students need to be able to understand and appreciate people who are different and communicate effectively with them. Such communication includes the ability to interact in multiple social settings.

Standards for Goal 3

Students will:

1. use the appropriate language variety, register, and genre according to audience, purpose, and setting

2. use nonverbal communication appropriate to audience, purpose, and setting

3. use appropriate learning strategies to extend their socio-linguistic and sociocultural competence

Word List

(* means irregular words—refer to page 118 for pronunciation)

a	Beth	chicken	drink	flute	guy/s*
above*	between*	class*	drive/s	fly/ies	gym*
after	big	classroom	drop	folk	hail
again	bird	classical	drum	food	happy*
age	bite	clear	dry/ies	fork	has*
all	black	clock	ear	forty	hat
and	blow/s	clothes*	earrings	four*	have*
angel*	blue	cloud	earphones	fourteen	he
animal	boat	clown	easy	fox*	head*
April	book*	coat	eat/s	Friday	heal
are	boots	coin	egg	frog	hear
arm	bounce*	cold	eight*	front	heavy*
around	box*	cool	eighteen	fruit	help/s
at	boy	come/s*	elephant	fun	her
away	bread*	corn	eleven	game	here
baby	brick	couch	else	garden	hey*
baby-sit	bright*	country*	eyes*	gas	hi
back	brother	cow	face*	gas pump	hide
backpack	brown	crab	fall*	get/s	high
bad	brush	crown	family	gift	hill*
bag	Bud	crutch/es	fan belt	girl	his
ball*	bug	cry/ies	farm	give	hit/s
ballad	bus	cube	fast	glad	hold/s
bananas*	but	cut	fat	glass/es	home plate
barn	by	dance	father	glue	home run
baseball	bye	dark	feel/s	go/goes	hoop
basketball	cage*	dash/es	feet	goat	hop/s
bat	cake	day	fence	gospel	hot
bath	can	deer	few	grain	house
bathroom	can't	desk	field	grandma	how
bathtub	cannot	diaper*	fifteen	grandmother	huge*
beach	cap	different	fifty	grandpa	hungry
beans	car	dining room	finally	grape/s	hurt/s
beard	cat	dish/es	fire	graph	I
bed	catch	do*	fish	grass	ice*
bedroom	CD	doctor	fit/s	gray	in
before	chair	dog	five	great*	in back of
behind	change*	don't*	flag	green	in front of
below	charge card	door*	flakes	ground	inside
belt	check	down	flat	group/s	is*
bend	cheese*	downtown	float/s	grow/s	isn't*
beside/s	chew	dress	floor	gum	**(continued on next page)**

it	mad	nose	problem	she	Steve
it's	mail box	not	purple	sheep	stick
its	Main	nothing	purse	shelf	still
jacket	make/s	now	quiz*	shine	stop/s
jazz	man	number	race	ship	store
jeans	many*	nurse	rain	shirt	stove
Jen	map	object	raincoat	shoe/s	street
jog/s	mat	o'clock*	rainy	shoot/s	string
joyful	match	of*	rap	shop/s	study
juice*	math	off*	read/s	show/s	summer
jump/s	May	office	red	side	sun
June	me	old	reggae	sign*	sunburn
keep/s	meat	on	rhyme/s*	sing/s	sunny
key	men	one*	ride	sister	sure
kind/s	metal	open	right	sit/s	swim/s
king	mice	other	right hand	six*	swollen
kitchen	midday	outside	ring	sixteen	table
knee	Mike	over	ripe	sixty	tail
knife	miles	page*	road	skin	tap
know	milk	pail	rock*	skirt	tan
lake	minus	pain	roof	sky	tattoo
land/s	minutes*	pan	rope	sled	team
last	mitt*	park	rose	sleep/s	teapots
lay/s	Monday	part	Roth	slow	tears
leaf	monkey	party/ies	round	smell	telephone
leave/s	month/s	past	rowboat	smile	ten
left	mop	Pat	rug	snack	tennis*
left hand	more	peach	rule	snail	tent
leg	mouse	peas	run/s	snake	test
let	mouth	pedal/s	sad	snow	that
let's	movies	pen	sale	soap	the*
life	mud	phonics	salsa	socks*	then
light	music	photo	same	soft	there*
like/s	my	pick-up truck	sand	song	these
lines	near	picnic	sandwich	sorry	they
little*	need	pie	say/s	sound/s	thick
live/s*	nest	pitch	school	soup	thin
living room	net	place	score	south	think/s
long	new	plane	scoreboard*	spill/s	thirteen
lot	next to	plant	scratch	splash/es	thirty
loud	nice	plate	sea	sports	this
love	night	play	see/s	stage	those
low	nine	plus	set/s	stand/s	three
luck	nineteen	pond	seven	star/s	throw
lunch	no*	pool	seventeen	start/s	thumb*
lunchbox	noise	pot	shake	stay	Thursday
Luz	noon	pretty	shave/s	step/s	time

(continued on next page)

tire/s	truck	use/s	waves	whistle*	years
to*	T-shirt	valley	weather	white	yell/s
toe/s	tub	van	wear/s*	wide	yellow
toilet	Tuesday	visit	Wednesday	Will	yes
Tom	tune	voice	well	wind (n)	yikes
tonight	TV	wait/s	west	window	you
top	twelve	wake/s up	wet	winter	your
town	twenty	walk/s*	whale	with	yourself
toy/s	two*	want*	what*	woman*	
train	umpire	wash/es	wheat	write	
tray	under	watch	wheel	wrong	
tree	up	water	when	X-ray	

The International Phonetic Alphabet

Consonants

/b/	baby, tub
/d/	down, today, sad
/f/	fun, off, phone, elephant
/g/	girl, big
/h/	home, behind
/k/	key, black, picnic
/l/	like, pail
/m/	mat, summer, swim
/n/	no, winter, pan
/ŋ/	sing
/p/	pot, purple, map
/r/	rain, around, door, write
/s/	sister, bus
/š/	she, fish
/t/	tent, little
/θ/	think, math
/ð/	this, clothes, brother
/v/	van, have, of
/w/	wave, one
/y/	yes
/z/	quiz, nose
/ž/	measure
/č/	check, watch
/ǰ/	job, cage

Vowels

/a/	on, hot, father
/æ/	hat, back
/ɛ/	egg, pen, says, head
/ɪ/	in, hill
/ɔ/	off, lot, cannot
/e/	make, train, say
/i/	see, read, key, field
/o/	open, rose, boat, slow
/ü/	flute, boot, do, you, fruit
/ʌ/	up, bus, of
/u/	put
/ə/	the, around
/ɚ/	mother, doctor
/ɝ/	her, bird, nurse

Diphthongs

/aɪ/	like, my, pie, night
/au/	out, down, how
/ɔɪ/	noise, boy

The English Alphabet

Here is the pronunciation of the letters of the English alphabet, written in International Phonetic Alphabet symbols.

a	/e/	j	/ǰe/	s	/ɛs/
b	/bi/	k	/ke/	t	/ti/
c	/si/	l	/ɛl/	u	/yu/
d	/di/	m	/ɛm/	v	/vi/
e	/i/	n	/ɛn/	w	/ˈdʌbəlˌyu/
f	/ɛf/	o	/o/	x	/ɛks/
g	/ǰi/	p	/pi/	y	/waɪ/
h	/eč/	q	/kyu/	z	/zi/
i	/aɪ/	r	/ar/		

Irregular Words

The following words, which are coded with an icon 🔑 in the text, represent either sight words or pronunciations which vary from the phonics rules specified in this book. They are listed with their phonetic spellings to help you pronounce them.

Key Words

above	əbʌv	juice	jŭs
ball/s	bɔl/z	lives	lɪvz
bananas	bənænəz	many	mɛni
bread	brɛd	minutes	mɪnəts
brown	braun	noises	nɔizəs
child	čaɪld	of	əʌ
clothes	kloz	page	peǰ
diaper	daɪpər	puts	puts
do	dü	rhyme/s	raɪm/z
don't	dont	scoreboard	skɔrbɔrd
door	dɔr	she	ši
eyes	aɪz	shoes	šüz
face	fes	sign	saɪn
fall/s	fɔl/z	sure	sɔ
four	fɔr	the	ðə
great	gret	thumb	θʌm
gym	jɪm	to	tü
has	hæz	two	tü
have	hæv	walk/s	wɔk/s
hey	he	want/s	want/s
house	haus	wash/es	waš/z
huge	hyuǰ	water	wɔtər
ice	aɪs	wear/s	wɛr/z
isn't	ɪzənt	whistle	hwɪsəl
joyful	jɔɪfəl		

Other Irregular Words

angel	enjəl	heavy	hɛvi
book	buk	is	ɪz
cheese	čiz	one	wʌ
come/s	kʌm/z	there	ðɛr
country	kʌntri	what	hwat
guy/s	gaɪ/z	woman	wumən
head	hɛd		

Index

Bibliography

Adams, M. J. 1990. *Beginning to Read: Thinking and Learning About Print.* Cambridge: Massachusetts Institute of Technology.

Blevins, W. 1998. *Phonics from A to Z: A Practical Guide.* New York: Scholastic.

Chall, J. and Popp, H., 1996. *Teaching and Assessing Phonics.* Cambridge, Massachusetts: Educators Publishing Service Inc.

Foorman, B. R., Francis, D. J., Fletcher, J. M., Schatschneider, C., and Mehta, P. 1998. "The Role of Instruction in Learning to Read: Preventing Reading Failure in At-Risk Children." *Journal of Educational Psychology* 90 (1–15).

Honig, B. 1996. *Teaching Our Children to Read: The Role of Skills in a Comprehensive Reading Program.* Thousand Oaks, CA: Corwin Press.

Moats, L. C. 1998. "Teaching Decoding." *American Educator* 22 (42–49) Washington, D.C.: The American Federation of Teachers, AFL-CIO.

Samuels, S. J. 1988. "Decoding and Automaticity: Helping Poor Readers Become Automatic at Word Recognition." *The Reading Teacher* (April).

Snider, V. E. 1995. "A Primer on Phonemic Awareness: What It Is, Why It's Important, and How to Teach It." *School Psychology Review* 24 (3)

Treiman, R., and Baron, J. 1981. "Segmental Analysis Ability: Development and Relation to Reading Ability." *Reading Research: Advances in Theory and Practice* (3).

Wiley, K. 1994. *Alligator at the Airport: A Language Activities Dictionary.* New York: Addison Wesley Longman, Inc.

Yopp, H. K. 1995. "Read-Aloud Books for Developing Phonemic Awareness: An Annotated Bibliography. *The Reading Teacher* 48 (6).